THE
Bourbon
COMPANION

THE Bourbon COMPANION

A Connoisseur's Guide

by Gary Regan

and

Mardee Haidin Regan

RUNNING PRESS

PHILADELPHIA · LONDON

To the Honorable Order of Kentucky Colonels

in the Commonwealth of Kentucky

and to all the bourbon lovers on Earth.

COLONEL
ALBERT BACON BLANTON

LOVED AND RESPECTED,
MASTER DISTILLER AND
TRUE KENTUCKY GENTLEMAN,
HE DEDICATED 55 YEARS

Printed in China

9   8   7   6   5   4   3   2   1
Digit on the right indicates the number of this printing

Library of Congress Cataloging-in-Publication Number 97-76135

ISBN 0-7624-0013-7

This book may be ordered by mail from the publisher.
Please include $2.50 for postage and handling.
But try your bookstore first!

Running Press Book Publishers
125 South Twenty-second Street
Philadelphia, Pennsylvania 19103-4399

CONTENTS

PART I

The Story
of
Bourbon

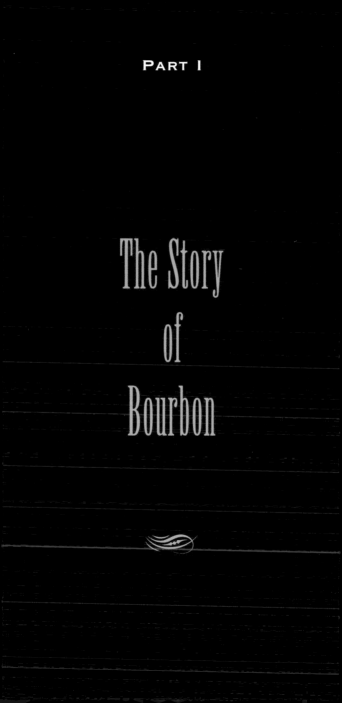

Introduction

Until very recently, if you ordered a shot of bourbon at your neighborhood tavern, the bartender most likely would reach for a shot glass and ask if you wanted a short beer on the side. Request a bourbon now and the barkeep will present you with a list of specialty bottlings, begin polishing a snifter—or if you're very lucky, a copita (a stovepipe-shaped sherry glass typically used for tasting)—and no doubt will strike up a conversation, asking whether you prefer a wheated bourbon or one made with rye as the secondary grain. Bourbon, the all-American spirit, following hot on the trail of single malt scotch, has finally come into its own.

Since the repeal of Prohibition in 1933, the American whiskey industry has metamorphosed into a far different business from that known to our turn-of-the-century forebears. Out of the hundreds of whiskey distilleries that were in operation prior to the Noble Experiment, fewer than a score remain today. However, in the late 1980s, a handful of huge corporations—United Distillers USA, The Sazerac Company, and the Jim Beam Brands Company, among them—began to introduce boutique bottlings of their finest American whiskeys. Now, in addition to our traditional brands of bourbons and Tennessee whiskeys, we have dozens of new bottlings of *"red likker"* with which to whet our collective whistle. Without question, this is the most exciting period for the American whiskey business since Jim Crow perfected the sour-mash process prior to the Civil War.

This phenomenon should come as no surprise to anyone who has insight into the soul of America. The United States is a country that seizes opportunity, and when the opportunity arises to make profit on a high-quality product, Americans are among the first to spare no expense in supplying the public demand. Look at the beer industry as an example: more than eight hundred brewpubs, micro-breweries, and craft breweries are now in operation, and we can choose from more than one thousand different brews. In 1978 there were fewer than ninety American breweries producing under twenty-five brands of beer. Americans are demanding high quality—and they are getting it.

The same is true of American whiskeys. Come with us,

then, on a journey of discovery. We will explain all the confusing terms that have been bandied about for the past couple of decades, show you how Americans make their whiskeys, tell you about the first whiskeys to be made on these shores, and bring you our notes and ratings on the best American whiskeys to be had. Discovering these whiskeys, and keeping up-to-date on this blossoming industry has been, for us, a wondrous affair. We hope that you, too, will marvel at the dedication, passion, and fervor of our American whiskey men and women. These are people who represent our country with pride in their hearts and a little whiskey in their blood.

DISTILLERY WORKERS AT CRYSTAL SPRINGS, 1886.

A BRIEF HISTORY

To discover what makes today's American whiskeys so different from those produced in Scotland, Ireland, or even Japan, we must take a glance at our earliest roots: Although the Pilgrims distilled rum from molasses imported from the West Indies and made wine from all manner of fruits that grew wild in the New World, their wines and spirits had no discernible style. American whiskey didn't start to develop any particular style at all until the 1700s, when half a million Germans and Scots-Irish immigrated to the East Coast—and more than a few had an intimate knowledge of the still. To their dismay, however, these farmer-distillers found that their beloved barley, from which many of them had been making whiskey for centuries, didn't fare too well on these shores.

Corn, however, grew wild all around. Yet since corn was new to them, and nonexistent in the Old World, the immigrants needed time and experience to understand how to use corn for food and eventually in their stills. Rye, on the other hand, was a grain the farmer-distillers knew well, and it took to American soil almost immediately. Thus, by the mid-1700s, American rye whiskey was born, and after winning the battle for representation to go along with taxation, these early whiskey men and women were about to discover just how tough taxation could be.

In 1791, President George Washington introduced excise taxes on spirits to offset America's considerable war debt. But the distillers simply refused to pay up. They couldn't understand why they should pay taxes on a homegrown product that was used more for bartering than for generating hard cash. They ranted and they raved, they burned down tax collectors' houses, they tarred and feathered the tax collectors themselves, and eventually, Washington was forced to call out federal troops for the first time in United States history. It was a bold move—he wasn't really sure that the troops would muster. But muster they did, and in 1794 Washington quelled the Whiskey Rebellion and secured his authority as Father of the Nation.

Meanwhile, many Americans began moving farther afield. Kentucky was originally part of Virginia, and by promising to build a cabin and grow corn, pioneers were granted land rights in what was to become the Bluegrass State. Many of the westward movers were the immigrant farmer-distillers from the East Coast, and because they were obliged to grow corn, they soon figured out how to use it to make whiskey.

By the late 1700s Kentuckians were shipping whiskey down the Ohio and Mississippi Rivers to New Orleans. The whiskey was shipped from Limestone, a riverside port in Bourbon County, Kentucky, and it soon became known as that whiskey from Bourbon. Eventually, just the word bourbon would suffice. If you had the opportunity to sample eighteenth-century bourbon from Kentucky, chances are good that you wouldn't recognize it. But if you were way down yonder in New Orleans, you might have found that the whiskey was a little smoother and bore a tinge of that familiar crimson hue peculiar to bourbon today. Why? Because it had spent time in oak barrels both immediately after it was made and for the several months required to ship it all the way down south. American distillers took note.

Many people claim that the Reverend Elijah Craig, a Baptist minister, was the first man to make bourbon, and indeed, this particular preacher did make whiskey that was probably known as bourbon back in the late 1700s. But was his whiskey aged, as our bourbons are today, in charred, brand-new, oak casks? It's doubtful. In fact, it took a Scot, Dr. James Crow, to insist on aging his whiskey that way, and Crow was also

ELIJAH CRAIG

responsible for perfecting the sour-mash method of whiskey-making. All this took place sometime between 1823 and, say, 1845.

So bourbon, as we know it, was born prior to America's Civil War, and although it has been through some changes along the way, it's still a true-blue American invention. In fact, in 1964, Congress declared bourbon to be a distinctive product of the United States, and therefore, although bourbon can be made anywhere in this country—Alaska, Hawaii, Maine, or Texas—no other country in the world is allowed to produce a whiskey called "bourbon."

It's easy to imagine the pride that those immigrant distillers of the 1700s would feel if they saw what had become of their tiny cottage industry. American whiskeys have been affected by all the trials and tribulations that have beset the nation as it struggled for its identity, and American whiskey has suffered the slings and arrows of fervid abolitionists, Prohibition, Repeal, and world war. But American whiskeys have lived long and prospered, unabashedly, our very own, true-blue all-American originals.

THE CRAFT OF MAKING AMERICAN WHISKEYS

While it can be said that some spirits—single malt scotch, rum, and cognac, among them—take on characteristics of their geographical location of manufacture, such is not at all the case with American whiskeys. More often differences among these all-American products result from the sometimes peculiar habits and customs of each distiller or distillery. Surprisingly enough, however, sometimes several entirely different bourbons will emanate from a single distillery.

Each distiller has two goals: to make sure that his or her whiskey doesn't taste like anyone else's, and that the nectar that is put in one bottle tastes different from other brands that wear different labels. Their techniques, of necessity, are many; after all, all bourbons and Tennessee whiskeys are made from just five ingredients—corn, rye or wheat, malted barley, yeast, and water—nothing else. The magic depends on producing a high-quality raw product and then controlling its nuances during its formative years in the barrel. A little bit of luck doesn't hurt a bit. Indeed, some masters of the craft aren't even sure why they do what they do; they do it because that's the way their daddies did it. Why play around with success?

TYPES OF WHISKEY

STRAIGHT WHISKEY

Most people we meet are unaware or confused about the difference between *straight* whiskeys and *blended* whiskeys. In fact, the two categories are very different from one another. Basically, putting the technical regulations aside for the moment, straight whiskeys are distilled from grains and have no other substances added to them (they can be diluted to bottling proof with water but that is the only allowable other component). Blended whiskeys comprise straight whiskeys that have had high-proof, characterless, neutral grain spirits added to them and often other colorings or flavorings. All of the whiskeys in this book are straight whiskeys. Here are the main points that differentiate straight whiskeys from their blended cousins. (We've added some explanations of what these rules mean to the consumer.)

STRAIGHT WHISKEY MUST:

• **Be distilled out (come out of its final distillation) at less than 80 percent alcohol by volume (abv).** The fact is, most American straight whiskeys run off the still at between 62.5 and 70 percent abv, and by keeping the proof low, the distillers ensure that more flavor stays in the whiskey. In comparison, vodka, which is meant to be flavorless, usually comes off the still at about 95 percent abv.

• **Be aged for a minimum of two years in new charred oak casks.** However, if the whiskey is matured for less than four years, its age must appear on the label. Therefore, most of the straight whiskey that appears on liquor store shelves is bound to be at least four years old. Many people think that whiskey must be aged in American white oak barrels, and indeed, all American whiskeys that we know of do spend their adolescence in that particular variety of oak since the configuration of the wood grain makes it ideal for holding liquid. But this is merely the choice of the distillers, no particular type of oak is specified in the law.

- **Contain no added coloring or flavoring.** When whiskey runs off the still it is clear—just like vodka—and it tastes similar to an eau-de-vie or any raw alcohol. But as the whiskey ages, certain impurities, known as congeners, react with the wood and develop into complex flavors within the spirit. The color of American straight whiskey is mostly a result of the spirit expanding into the barrel's charred wooden interior during the warmer months and gaining color from the so-called red layer in the barrel.

POT STILL DOUBLER AT THE NOW-CLOSED STITZEL-WELLER DISTILLERY.

BOURBON MASH FERMENTING AT THE MAKER'S MARK DISTILLERY

When the barrels are formed, the staves, or wood slats, are heated to help them bend, and the heat caramelizes some of the wood sugars and tannins within each stave. This toasting stage of the coopering process forms the red layer, which not only helps give color to the whiskey, but also imparts some extra flavors. After the barrels are assembled, their interiors are set afire over open flame creating a layer of charcoal over the red layer. When the whiskey is in the aging houses, it filters through that charcoal as it expands and contracts with seasonal temperature changes, or in certain cases, by artificially raising and lowering the temperature in the warehouse. Both the red layer and the charred interior add flavors to the whiskey.

Corn whiskey, which can be designated as a straight whiskey, differs from the regulations above only inasmuch as, if aged at all, it must be aged in either previously used charred oak barrels or new uncharred oak barrels.

SOUR-MASH WHISKEY

Sometime after 1823 a Scottish distiller by the name of Dr. James Crow (creator of Old Crow bourbon) perfected a seemingly peculiar but eminently practical method of making whiskey. After the first distillation had taken place, he drained the liquid from the leftover mash of fermented, cooked grains and then added a portion of this liquid to the mash of cooked grains and yeast that would be used for his next batch. (Crow also insisted on aging his whiskey in charred oak barrels—we think of him as the father of bourbon as we know it.) We look on sour mash, also called backset, as whiskey DNA—it brings the character of the previous batch of whiskey into the new mash, and is used to control the acidity of the mash and create a perfect environment for the temperamental new yeast.

Most American straight whiskeys, whether the words "sour mash" appear on the label or not, are made by the sour-mash method. Some companies have included it in a brand name and others don't even bother to mention it; nonetheless, virtually all of it is sour-mash whiskey.

STRAIGHT BOURBON

Because of a congressional proclamation issued in 1964, bourbon must be made in the United States. But it doesn't have to be made in Bourbon County, Kentucky (where there

CHARCOAL MELLOWING PROCESS AT THE JACK DANIEL DISTILLERY.

are no distilleries at present), or even in the state of Kentucky. Straight bourbon must be made with a minimum of 51 percent corn; the amounts of other grains are unspecified.

TENNESSEE WHISKEY

In practice, the two Tennessee whiskeys on the market today (George Dickel and Jack Daniel's) could be called bourbons since all of the bottlings conform to the rules and regulations that govern bourbon. Nearly

HOSING DOWN THE BURNING RICKS AT JACK DANIEL.

everyone thinks of Tennessee whiskey as bourbon—and calls it bourbon—yet Tennessee distillers dictate it be called Tennessee whiskey, a straight whiskey made in Tennessee. Besides its state of origin, the major difference between Tennessee whiskeys and bourbons is the charcoal-mellowing process that makes Tennessee whiskey taste so very different.

In the 1820s there lived in Lincoln County, Tennessee, a distiller by the name of Alfred Eaton, and he is said to be the man who first discovered that when he filtered his new whiskey through giant vats of sugar-maple charcoal, it became a much smoother product. Bear in mind that back in those days, whiskey usually wasn't aged at all; so, any process that took the rough edges off new whiskey was very desirable. The key thing to remember about Tennessee whiskey is that it undergoes its mellowing prior to aging.

Eaton's procedure is now known as the "Lincoln County Process," "charcoal leaching," or "charcoal mellowing." We have tasted Tennessee whiskey straight off the still, and then again, after the mellowing process, and can vouch for the fact that it is this leaching through sugar-maple charcoal that gives the Tennessee product the wonderful sooty sweetness that is not present in bourbons. Though your bottle of bourbon may bear the words "charcoal filtered," the process is different from the

Lincoln County Process and is performed after aging and just before bottling. (See Filtration, page 31.)

STRAIGHT RYE WHISKEY

When Prohibition was repealed in December 1933, many whiskey drinkers were looking for the pure rye whiskey that

EXTRACTING A SAMPLE OF WHISKEY FOR TASTING.

had been so popular before the Noble Experiment. However, since distillation had been, for the most part, banned for almost fourteen years, there wasn't enough aged product on hand at the American distilleries. Enter the Canadian whisky distillers. Pioneers such as Joseph E. Seagram and Hiram Walker had plenty of blended Canadian whisky on hand, and it was common at the time for the Canadians to use a fair amount of rye in their production. As time went by, these blended Canadian whiskies became known as rye whiskies, and to a great extent, Americans lost their taste for straight rye whiskey.

Straight rye whiskey must adhere to the straight whiskey regulations noted above, and must be made from a mash that contains a minimum of 51 percent rye grain. Most straight ryes, however, are made with over 65 percent rye. Ryes are delicate, yet peppery, and far different from either blended whiskies or their bourbon cousins. Indeed, rye whiskeys were the favored dram of Americans in the mid-1700s, almost fifty years before Kentucky bourbon hit the scene.

SINGLE-BARREL WHISKEY

Single-barrel whiskeys are just that, the product of just one barrel of whiskey. These barrels, however, tend to be selected very carefully from prime areas of the warehouses since the distiller doesn't have the luxury of marrying one barrel with another to achieve a particular result. Each bottle of a single-barrel bourbon may differ slightly from the last barrel that was bottled—it is from a different barrel (check the label, the barrel number should be noted)—but each master distiller selects whiskeys that have matured into a specific flavor profile, and are, therefore, very similar to one another.

EVAN WILLIAMS SINGLE BARREL VINTAGE WHISKEY IS ONE DISTILLER'S RESPONSE TO THE EVER-GROWING CONSUMER DEMAND FOR SPECIAL BOTTLINGS.

SMALL-BATCH WHISKEY

This term has been the source of much confusion since most bourbon lovers believe that "small batch" denotes whiskey that has been distilled in small quantities. But that isn't true. In fact, small-batch whiskeys are the result of another side of the distiller's craft altogether. The term was introduced in the late 1980s by the Jim Beam Brands Company, and according to them, the term applies to "rare and exceptional Bourbons married from a cross section of barrels in the rack house." Fact is, different sections of a bourbon warehouse produce different whiskeys—most of the buildings are between seven and twelve stories tall, and since the temperatures differ on each level (progressively hotter toward the top), the whiskeys mature at different rates. Distillers of small-batch whiskeys select barrels that have aged into particular styles and mingle them together to achieve consistency. Since not many barrels mature into a style consistent with the quality that these distillers seek, they are, indeed, "rare and exceptional."

Having said that, however, we must point out that there are many rare and exceptional bourbons out there that aren't designated as "small batch" bottlings, simply because the producers shy away from a phrase that might confuse their products with those from another company.

VINTAGE WHISKEY

At the time of writing, the Evan Williams Vintage Bourbon is the only vintage-dated bottling on the market. It is also a single-barrel bourbon. The only real difference here is that the distiller has chosen to note the date of distillation on the label, signifying that this is a special selection that is worthy of note. We have only one small quibble with the Evan Williams vintage bottling: Each bottle bears the date on which it was distilled, but not the date on which it was bottled—we want to know the age of the whiskey. (For the record, this whiskey is a very respectable eight years old and a darned fine bourbon to boot.)

MICRO-WHISKEY

There is, at this time, just one American whiskey designated as a "micro whiskey," and this bottling—Jacob's Well—goes through a process known as "double barreling." After the barrels of whiskey selected for this bottling are mingled together, the resultant whiskey is returned to the wood for further aging.

THE COMPONENTS OF
AMERICAN WHISKEY

GRAIN

Although corn must be the predominant grain (a minimum of 51 percent by law) in bourbon, most distillers use upward of 70 percent corn. The remaining 30 percent of the grain mixture, called the "small grains," is determined by each individual distiller. He or she can elect to use rye, the more traditional secondary grain, or wheat in addition to the malted barley that is essential to making the whole fermentation process begin. We have found that, to our tastes, whiskeys made

A TRUCK LOAD OF FOOD-GRADE CORN FOR JACK DANIEL DISTILLERY.

ANTIQUE YEAST COOLER.

with rye tend to be spicier than those made with wheat, which seems to offer a smoothness and elegance that we find fetching. Thus, we refer to whiskeys made with wheat rather than rye as "wheated bottlings."

"Mashbill" is the term applied to the grain recipe for each whiskey. It is usually expressed as a percentage, such as 72 percent corn, 16 percent rye, and 12 percent barley malt. Some distilleries use the same mashbill to produce all of their raw whiskeys; others have different mashbills for different brands.

YEAST

All bourbon distillers are proud of their yeast strain and take great pains to guard its identity and ensure its uniqueness. They can buy commercially produced yeasts or cultivate their own on the premises. Every strain of yeast, though, adds its own properties to the final product. Indeed, those who cultivate their own yeast use some very strange methods to propagate the lifeblood of their whiskey. The Heaven Hill, Maker's Mark, and Jim Beam distilleries, for instance, all add hops to the cooked mixture of grains in which their yeast grows. Old Forester and Wild Turkey bourbons, on the other hand, use lactic bacteria to "sour" their sweet yeast mashes.

WATER

We would love to be able to tell you that all American whiskey producers insist on using pure spring water, filtered by the limestone shelf that lies beneath huge areas of Kentucky and Tennessee, but that simply isn't the case. Some distilleries go to enormous expense in order to pipe water from nearby springs into their fermenters, but some use city water, and still others use river water.

However, always remember that we are living in a technological age. It's fairly easy to treat city water or river water until it resembles the makeup of spring water, and this is the practice used by some distilleries (and much of the brewing industry) that don't have access to fresh, pure, spring water. Whatever its source or treatment, water is key to the whiskey-making process.

OTHER INFLUENCES ON AMERICAN WHISKEY

PROOF

In the United States, the "proof" of a spirit is expressed in degrees and is equal to double the percentage of beverage alcohol in the spirit. Therefore, if a bottle of whiskey is 100° proof, it contains 50 percent alcohol. An 86°-proof whiskey contains 43 percent alcohol, and so on.

In addition to the mashbill and yeast, the proof, that is, the percentage of alcohol by volume, at which the whiskey runs off its second (or third) distillation contributes greatly to the flavor of any whiskey. In general, the lower the proof, the more robust the whiskey will be. This, however, is a costly proposition for the distiller. Imagine how many bottles of 80°-proof whiskey a distiller could get out of a gallon of 160°-proof (the highest proof at which straight American whiskey can be distilled) spirit as compared to the number of bottles

ROLLING OUT THE BARRELS AT OLD FITZGERALD.

CHARCOAL MELLOWING VATS AT JACK DANIEL.

that could be filled from, say, a gallon of whiskey that leaves the still at around 125° proof. Luckily for us, however, American distillers know that flavorful whiskey will keep their customers returning for more. Therefore, most whiskeys made in the United States come off the still at around 125° proof.

AGING

The aging process also differentiates one whiskey from the next to an enormous degree, and it is during this maturing period that two barrels of whiskey, filled from a single distillation, can emerge just a few years later, as kinfolk, but certainly not twins.

In order to be called straight whiskey or straight bourbon, the new spirit must be aged in brand-new charred oak barrels, and although this law doesn't apply to other American whiskeys, including Tennessee whiskeys, it is, more or less, the norm throughout the American whiskey industry. The new barrels, therefore, usually made from American white oak, actually have their interiors set on fire in order to achieve the charred quality that is required by law. The fire is doused in less than a minute, but depending on how long the cooper lets the flames burn, varying degrees of char can be attained.

Each distiller can choose the degree of char, on a scale of

from one to four, that the cooperage puts on his barrels, and those who choose a deeper char swear it adds extra character to their whiskeys. But when those barrels are laid down for aging, a transformation takes place.

Most bourbon warehouses built from metal, brick, or wood are completely unheated, and are over eight stories tall. In the warm summer months, the whiskey that ages in barrels located at the top of these gigantic structures where temperatures are highest, matures much more quickly than those in the shaded, and relatively cooler, lower floors. Similarly, whiskey in casks by a window where the morning sun beams down will bear characteristics not found in whiskey aged in the dark depths of the center of the warehouse. Some, but relatively few, distilleries actually rotate their barrels, making sure that each cask gets its fair share of each part of the warehouse, but this is an expensive proposition, and most distillers simply marry whiskeys from each level to arrive at a consistent product. And just a few distilleries actually repeatedly

SUGAR-MAPLE CHARCOAL THAT WILL FLAVOR JACK DANIEL'S TENNESSEE WHISKEY.

heat their warehouses and then allow them to cool during the cooler months on the theory that these conditions speed up the maturation process.

However, when distillers bottle their whiskeys under different labels, they must make sure that each one fits its individual flavor profile. This is achieved by choosing, say, three casks from the top of the warehouse, one from the center, and four from the bottom to make one style of whiskey, and then, by altering the proportions from each area, making an entirely different bourbon—from the same initial whiskey.

UNDERSTANDING AMERICAN-WHISKEY TERMS

Some of the terms seen on labels of American whiskeys can be a little confusing, and new terms are often created either to meet governmental labeling regulations or, as is more often the case, for marketing purposes. The term "small batch" is probably the most misunderstood of the bunch, and although it is now used by companies other than the one that originally coined the phrase (The Jim Beam Brands Company), and seems to mean different things to each distillery, we should give this term the credit it deserves—it served to raise the curiosity of American whiskey lovers worldwide.

Here we present all the terms that you are likely to encounter when trying to choose among different bottlings of American whiskeys, and also a few pointers that will serve you well when discussing this category with others.

AGE STATEMENTS

The age on any bottle of American whiskey denotes the age of the youngest whiskey in the bottle; older whiskeys can be, and often are, added.

BOTTLED IN BOND

The Bottled-in-Bond Act of 1897 states that distillers can store their barrels of straight whiskey in government-supervised warehouses for a period of at least four years without paying taxes on the whiskey. After the aging period, the whiskey must be bottled at 50-percent abv or 100° proof. As a result of the government guarantee, bottled-in-bond whiskeys became very popular spirits in the early twentieth

TURN-OF-THE-CENTURY BONDED BOURBON WAREHOUSE.

century, and to this day, some consumers tend to look on the term as an endorsement of quality. In practice, though, any straight whiskey bottled at 100° proof and without displaying an age statement (thus denoting a minimum of four years in the wood) is of a similar caliber.

FILTRATION

Most American whiskeys—in fact Booker's bourbon is the only exception that we know—are filtered after aging and before bottling with activated charcoal. Some are filtered at room temperature, others are chilled and then filtered, but the process is quick and meant solely to remove certain impurities that affect the visual appeal of the whiskey. No flavor is imparted by activated charcoal. Why do it? Because when unfiltered whiskey gets too cold, it can develop a "chill haze" or cloudiness. There's nothing wrong with cloudy whiskey, in fact, it is generally more flavorful than the filtered variety, but the public at large doesn't know that. They think the whiskey is spoiled in some way and don't want to buy it; therefore, distillers generally filter their bourbon before bottling it. Tennessee whiskey goes through the same quick filtration process after aging.

HOW AMERICAN WHISKEY IS MADE

• Grains, usually around 75% corn, 15% rye or wheat, and 10% malted barley, are cooked in a mash tub and transferred to a fermenter.

• Yeast—either a specific strain of dried yeast, or one cultivated from the distiller's own strain of "jug yeast"—is added to the fermenter. The yeast acts on the fermentable sugars in the mash and converts them into beverage alcohol, carbon dioxide, and heat.

If the whiskey being made is sour-mash whiskey (and most American whiskeys are), then some backset—the thin, watery part of the residue taken from the still after a previous distillation—is also added to the fermenter with the yeast. The acid content of backset allows the distiller to alter the pH level of the mash and also carries some of the characteristics of the previous batch through to the new mash.

• After the mash has fermented for three or four days and the alcohol level has reached about 8 percent (abv), the mash is now called "distiller's beer." This beer is entered into a still (usually, but not always, a continuous still) where it will be distilled into "low wines" or "singlings."

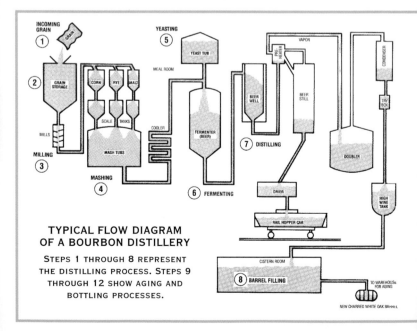

TYPICAL FLOW DIAGRAM OF A BOURBON DISTILLERY

STEPS 1 THROUGH 8 REPRESENT THE DISTILLING PROCESS. STEPS 9 THROUGH 12 SHOW AGING AND BOTTLING PROCESSES.

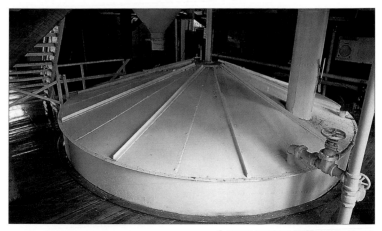

A GRAIN COOKER AT MAKER'S MARK.

• The low wines, relatively low in alcohol, are usually redistilled in a doubler—a type of pot still—or a thumper. A thumper looks a lot like a doubler—sort of a tin can with a Hershey's Kiss topknot, but it contains water through which the low wines, in vapor form, are bubbled. Since the low wines aren't condensed until after their journey through the thumper (which thumps as the vapors pass through

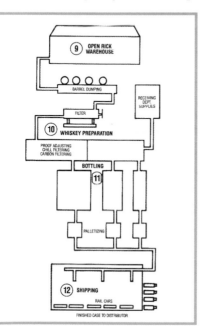

the water), this isn't technically a redistillation, but the process does purify the spirit somewhat. When condensed, the spirit from the doubler or thumper is known as "high wines" or "doublings."

• The high wines are then entered into charred, new, white oak barrels where they will mature for some years to come.

Note: Some of the newer distilleries are currently employing pot stills to make their American whiskeys; the ones that do are noted in the distillery section.

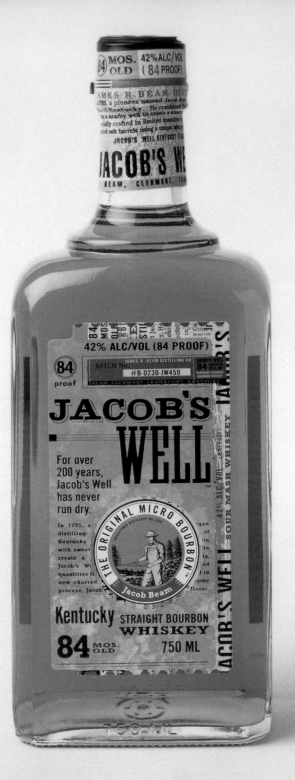

THE ART OF APPRECIATING AMERICAN WHISKEY

To truly appreciate the king of American whiskeys, you have to understand that not all bourbon drinkers want a deep, somber whiskey all of the time; remember, bourbon is American, and the style of the whiskey has developed alongside the American predilection for iced drinks. Some enjoy their favorite tot on the rocks, and many people are prone to adding flavored or neutral mixers to their bourbon. Unlike their Scottish counterparts, however, bourbon distillers aren't likely to kick and scream when they see their whiskey being mixed with just about anything. Personally, although we generally favor American whiskey neat—without ice—we also enjoy different styles of bourbon for different occasions: medium-bodied, full-flavored whiskeys in a Manhattan cocktail; light, crisp bottlings in a Mint Julep; and sometimes we even select a lean, mean whiskey to mix with ginger ale as the sun beats down on our fevered brows.

But for serious whiskey tasting that allows you to savor the intricacies, you should sip it at room temperature from a glass with a wider base than the rim—copitas (stovepipe-shaped sherry glasses) are the choice among most professional tasters. You might want to taste the whiskey neat initially, and then add a small proportion of bottled water (spring water or branch water) to dilute the whiskey, and taste it again. A whole new set of aromas and flavors can be released with the addition of a little spring water.

COMING TO YOUR SENSES

Bourbon is made in many different styles: lean, light, and masculine; deep, heavy, and buxom; stouthearted and bold, but never meek and mild. The best bourbons, of course, are those that lend themselves to a snifter—the whiskeys that need nothing but the warmth of your hand cupped around the bowl. You might want to add a splash of spring water to some overproof bottlings, but we recommend that you first taste your whiskey neat and then decide whether or not to add water.

Having said that, you should also be aware that some snifter-quality, heavy-bodied bourbons don't necessarily lend themselves well to Mint Juleps; we recommend lighter, more aromatic whiskeys for that particular cocktail. You must also bear in mind that bourbon is an American whiskey, and whereas the average Scot will most likely tear your arm from its socket at the mention of a single malt cocktail, Kentuckians are quite fond of Manhattans and a few other straight bourbon-based cocktails. This whiskey grew up in America—the birthplace of the cocktail.

EYES

Unlike many brown spirits, cognacs among them, no coloring of any sort can be added to straight American whiskey. So your first clue as to the character of a straight whiskey is in its hue. Some bourbons are distinctively red—Old Grand-Dad 114° proof is a great example—while others appear to have a tinge of red or are better described as amber. Don't dismiss the amber bourbons out of hand, although the color is a good initial clue to the character of the whisky, the real test comes in the aromas and palate.

NOSE

Vanilla is often the first scent to waft gently to your nose as you savor your bourbon; lighter-bodied bottlings may also bear aromatic herbal or floral qualities, such as wildflowers, grass, and/or clover. The heavier bourbons, however, usually bear a sweet fruitiness, varying in intensity from tangerine to caramelized oranges or from sweet plums to over-ripe blueberries.

MOUTH

Good whiskey is well-bred. It will never scorch your palate or tear apart your throat. Look for the same flavors described in the Nose section above, but now you should also be observing what the whiskey does to your mouth. The best snifter-quality bourbons will bear a huge body that fills your mouth with soft velvet and coats your entire palate with an intense burst of vanilla, butter, and deep, dark fruits.

THROAT

The finish of a good whiskey should be lingering and

warm, although some of the lighter bottlings tend to have a wonderful spiciness—these are the whiskeys to savor on the rocks.

MAKING BOURBON COCKTAILS AND MIXED DRINKS

Because bourbon is the quintessential American spirit, it's only natural that it's also a perfect base for another homebred creation—the cocktail. Cocktails have been around since the end of the eighteenth century, and the whole world agrees that we owe their invention to American ingenuity. Here we detail four classic bourbon-based drinks, and although we love to sip our bourbon neat, we also end almost every workday with one of these cocktails or mixed drinks. (Okay, it's usually a Manhattan.)

THE MANHATTAN

The Manhattan was born in the 1870s at a banquet hosted by Lady Jenny Churchill in honor of Samuel J. Tilden, a prominent lawyer of the time, at New York City's Manhattan Club, and as we detailed in our book, *The Martini Companion*, we believe that the Manhattan was actually responsible for the creation of the Dry Martini. It's a long, complicated story, but suffice it to say that, according to the scores of cocktail books dating back to 1862 that we referenced, the

THE MANHATTAN, A FIRESIDE FAVORITE.

Manhattan spawned the Martinez, which became known as the Martini, which in turn, gave birth to the Dry Martini.

There are two very important aspects to remember when making a Manhattan: First, if it doesn't contain bitters (Angostura, Peychaud, or orange), it isn't a Manhattan. Second, the proportion of bourbon to sweet vermouth is of tantamount importance. However, there is no hard-and-fast rule governing these proportions since, depending on the brand of bourbon you select, you might decide to add more—or less—bourbon than we recommend here. The key is experimentation, but you should always remember that you are not making a Martini and therefore, a goodly amount of sweet vermouth (at least one-fourth of the entire drink) is mandatory. If we have more than one Manhattan, we often choose to use more vermouth in our second drinks just to cut back a little on the alcohol content. Here's a basic recipe, but we urge you to play around with the proportions until you find your own favorite.

> **2** OUNCES STRAIGHT BOURBON
> **1** OUNCE SWEET VERMOUTH
> **2** DASHES BITTERS (ANGOSTURA OR ORANGE
>   BITTERS ARE TRADITIONAL, BUT PEYCHAUD
>   MAKES FOR AN INTERESTING VARIATION)
> **1** MARASCHINO CHERRY

Chill a stemmed cocktail glass of your choice (a common pick is the martini glass). Pour the whiskey, vermouth, and bitters into a mixing glass half-filled with ice cubes. Stir well for 20 to 30 seconds. Strain the mixture into the chilled cocktail glass. Garnish with the maraschino cherry.

THE MINT JULEP, PERFECT FOR SUMMER.

THE MINT JULEP

Even in Louisville, most people drink Mint Juleps only on Kentucky Derby Day, but after consulting Richard Barksdale Harwell's 1975 book, *The Mint Julep*, we have found one more appropriate day of the year on which to sip this incredible drink—June 1st. Harwell quotes a certain Theodore Irwin who wrote that the Mint Julep was introduced to students at Oxford University in 1874 by a South Carolinian named William Heyward

Trapier. And to this day, Oxford students at New College make this drink annually on June 1st, in honor of Trapier's visit. We cheat a little by serving Juleps on the first Sunday of June since, if the first day of that month lands on, say, a Wednesday, there would be no work achieved at all on that day.

The biggest controversy surrounding the Mint Julep lies in the question of whether or not mint leaves should be crushed into the bottom of the glass before the drink is made, and although we have savored Juleps made that way and loved every drop, when we make Mint Juleps, the only mint you'll see will be sitting atop of the drink as a treat for your nose as you sip sweetened bourbon through the straw. Here's our favorite recipe.

2 CUPS FINELY CRUSHED ICE

2 OUNCES BOURBON

$^3/_4$ OUNCE SIMPLE SYRUP

1 FRESH MINT BOUQUET, THE STEMS CUT SHORT AT THE LAST POSSIBLE MOMENT

1. Fill a tall glass (silver julep cup if you have one) two-thirds full with crushed ice. Add the bourbon and syrup; stir for 20 seconds to blend.

2. Add more crushed ice until the ice mounds over the rim of the cup. Stir gently for about 20 seconds. Garnish with the whole bouquet of mint. Insert 2 straws that have been cut short so that the ends just about reach over the top of the mint.

3. Allow the Julep to stand until a thin sheath of ice forms on the outside of the cup. Serve with a cocktail napkin to catch the condensation.

THE FLAVORFUL OLD FASHIONED.

THE OLD FASHIONED

The Old Fashioned was reportedly created at Louisville's Pendennis Club, and it was introduced to New York by Colonel James E. Pepper, a famed nineteenth-century bourbon distiller. Some people like to muddle the fruit with the bitters and sugar in the bottom of the glass while others use the fruit simply as a garnish. We are of the muddling school.

1 ORANGE SLICE, CUT $^1/_2$-INCH THICK

1 MARASCHINO CHERRY

3 DASHES BITTERS (ANGOSTURA IS TRADITIONAL
BUT PEYCHAUD OR ORANGE BITTERS MAKE FOR
INTERESTING VARIATIONS)

1 TEASPOON WATER

$^1/_2$ TEASPOON SUPERFINE SUGAR

2$^1/_2$ OUNCES BOURBON

In a double old-fashioned glass, combine the orange slice, cherry, bitters, water, and sugar. Using a wooden pestle or the back of a teaspoon, carefully muddle the ingredients until the sugar dissolves and the fruit is thoroughly crushed. Fill the glass with ice cubes. Add the bourbon and stir gently.

SOME FRESH LEMON <u>MAKES</u> A WHISKEY SOUR.

THE WHISKEY SOUR

At the time of writing, it was just yesterday when we were sipping scotch sours with our new friend Helen Anne, but usually, in the warmer months, we sip bourbon sours as the sun beats down on our fevered brows. Bourbon sours are at once refreshing and dangerous—they'll quench your thirst and make you want a second and a third quite rapidly, but be careful, a good bourbon sour contains a healthy shot of whiskey. (You can alter the amount of simple syrup to suit your taste.)

2 1/2 OUNCES BOURBON
1 1/2 OUNCES FRESH LEMON JUICE
1/2 OUNCE SIMPLE SYRUP
1 ORANGE SLICE
1 MARASCHINO CHERRY

In a shaker half-filled with ice cubes, combine the bourbon, lemon juice, and simple syrup. Shake well until very cold. Strain into a whiskey sour glass or a champagne flute. Garnish with the orange slice and cherry.

Stock This!
"The Oldest and Best Brand made in Kentucky"
GUARANTY
BOTTLED IN BOND
JAMES E. PEPPER
ESTABLISHED 1780
BORN WITH THE REPUBLIC
PEPPER DISTILLERY
WHISKEY
LEXINGTON, KY.
STATE OF KENTUCKY
JAS. E. PEPPER & CO.
"Born with the Republic"
BOTTLED IN BOND
Jas. E. Pepper & Co.
Distillers
Lexington, Ky.

PART II

A - Z Directory
of
American Whiskeys

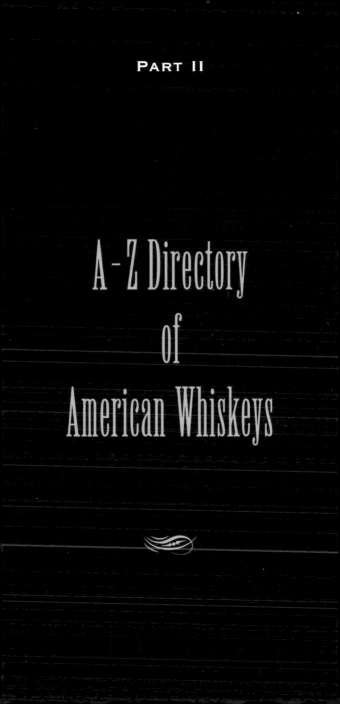

OLD CHARTER ADVERTISEMENT FROM 1973.

NOTES ON THE TASTING NOTES

You will notice that many of the whiskeys in this chapter emanate from the same distilleries, and some plants put out as many as ten different brand names. However, although some of the less expensive bottlings may contain the same whiskey but bear a different name, on the whole, most of the distilleries choose aged spirits from different barrels and mingle them to fit the flavor profile of each label.

This procedure is a very complicated affair: The distiller tastes samples from barrels located in different sections of the warehouses and identifies which whiskeys should be used for which bottling. But since most of these warehouses are several stories high and have huge variances in location, temperature, and humidity between the lower levels and the top floors, each barrel matures at its own rate. Thus, the distiller has access to a wide range of flavors that can be mingled together in order to meet specifications.

Notes on the Ratings

We conducted blind tastings of all the whiskeys in this chapter; the resultant notes and ratings are a compilation of both our findings. Rating whiskeys is a difficult task, and many factors come into play—time of day, mood, personal likes and dislikes, and so forth. Tasting is very subjective. And because the price differences among these bottlings can be vast—$10 to more than $100—it's important to take the expense of a bottle into account. Where appropriate, we have noted that some bottlings are reasonably priced or good for the price. For example, isn't a bourbon that scores 84 and sells for $12 worth a try when compared to one that rates the same score but costs twice as much?

Flavors and aromas mentioned in these notes can prove confusing to some, but there is no appropriate way to describe any distilled spirit other than by mentioning specific herbs, spices, fruits, and other nuances that we detect when tasting professionally. Don't be put off if you don't detect the same specific flavors as we do, that's okay. The real question is: Do *you* like it?

Although many of the pricier bottlings are meant to be of high enough quality to be served neat at room temperature, it's important to remember that many bourbons are specifically designed for all-around use—in mixed drinks and cocktails, straight up or on the rocks. With this in mind, take a look at the overall category at the end of each set of tasting notes. This category is more important than either the flavor profile or the ratings of each whiskey; you'll get a clear picture of how we view each bottling.

If we recommend that you sip a certain whiskey neat (without ice), you'll know that we hold it in very high regard, and similarly, because we are both devoted to Manhattan cocktails, you'll know that if we suggest the whiskey can be used to construct a Manhattan, it rates high on our list. Bottlings that we advise should be consumed on the rocks, with water, or with club soda fall a little lower on our list, and those whiskeys that we tell you to use solely for mixed drinks fall lower still. Combinations of these suggestions, on the rocks or in mixed drinks, for example, tell you that the whiskey lies somewhere between those categories.

The ratings themselves, however, tell you our view of the

whiskey when tasted twice: first, neat and at room temperature, and then second, with a few drops of bottled water added. The ratings assigned to each whiskey refer to our opinion of how well the whiskey is crafted, and once again we should note that the overall category will prove most useful for consumers. Here's how the numbers work:

96+.	Excellent
91–95	Highly recommended
86–90	Recommended
81–85	Good
76–80	Fair
75 and below	Poor

How to Use this Directory

Contrary to all of the strictly proper ways of alphabetizing, we have found that being absolutely literal is the way to go with listings as odd as these. The whiskeys that follow are listed in strict alphabetical sequence; using the first letter of the first word in each bottling's name. So, for example, A. H. Hirsch bottlings are listed under *A*; Jim Beam is under *J*—not *B*. For the most part, this method makes finding a particular bottling simple, but readers who enjoy, say, Barton's bourbons, should remember that their whiskeys are called Very Old Barton, and will be found under *V*, as opposed to *B*.

A. H. Hirsch Bourbon

Distillery: Michter's, near Shaefferstown, Pennsylvania (now closed)

Merchants: Cork n Bottle, Covington, Kentucky

The Whiskey: This bourbon was made in the early 1970s at the now-closed Michter's Distillery in Pennsylvania. Although it is designated as a pot-stilled bourbon, the pot still was used only for the secondary distillation; the primary distillation, as with the vast majority of whiskeys in this book, was performed in a continuous still. Having said that, however, it should be noted that the smaller, more labor-intensive pot stills, when used at whatever point in the process, are sure to make a difference—usually beneficial—to the resultant whiskey.

RESERVE
Pot-Stilled Sour Mash
Straight Bourbon Whiskey

16 YEARS OLD
Distilled in the Spring of 1974
Bottled by Hirsch Distillers
Lawrenceburg, Kentucky

45.8% Alc/Vol | 91.6 Proof | 750 ml

A. H. Hirsch Reserve Pot-Stilled Sour Mash Straight Bourbon
16 years old, 45.8% ABV

Rating: 92

A light, fragrant nose with unmistakable sandalwood notes and hints of old leather; big body with a fruity sweetness on the palate and a dash of sandalwood as a lighter backdrop; the finish is very long.

Overall: This bourbon, at 16 years old, is best served neat. It's clear proof that American bourbon can stand, and benefit from, extra time in the wood.

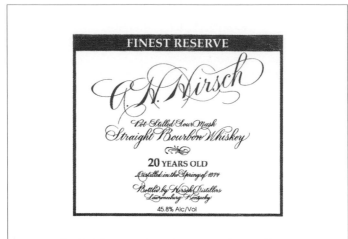

FINEST RESERVE

A. H. Hirsch

Pot-Stilled Sour Mash
Straight Bourbon Whiskey

20 YEARS OLD

Distilled in the Spring of 1974

Bottled by Hirsch Distillers
Lawrenceburg, Kentucky

45.8% Alc/Vol

A. H. HIRSCH POT-STILLED SOUR MASH STRAIGHT BOURBON
20 YEARS OLD, 45.8% ABV

RATING: 94

A complex nose that neatly balances caramel sweetness with a backdrop of fresh mint; the elegant, huge, syrupy body coats the mouth, and the palate offers a complex mélange of sweet vanilla, toffee, a sturdy oakiness, and a host of peppery spices; the finish is very long and very memorable.

Overall: Another whiskey best reserved for post-prandial consumption when it should always be served neat. Sip this fine bottling in good health.

American Biker Bourbon

DISTILLERY: Unknown (bottled by American Spirits International, Bardstown, Kentucky)

THE WHISKEY: Obviously directed toward the motorcycle crowd, this is a medium-priced whiskey that's very well packaged.

AMERICAN BIKER SOUR MASH BOURBON
43% ABV

RATING: 82

Sweet caramel nose with a barely detectable chocolate note; the body wavers between light and medium, and the palate, though simple, is pleasingly spicy, as is the relatively short finish.

Overall: A good bourbon for the price. Drink it on the rocks.

Ancient Age Bourbon

DISTILLERY: The Ancient Age Distillery, Leestown, Kentucky

THE WHISKEY: Ancient Age was initially released in 1936 as a bourbon-style blended whiskey. It was made in Canada and released to supply the huge demand for whiskey that followed Repeal. All Ancient Age bottlings are now true Kentucky bourbons and have been since shortly after the end of World War II. Although the brand isn't known as well as some of the newer boutique bottlings, there are folk in Kentucky who never drink anything else.

Although the distillery that makes Ancient Age is often referred to as the Blanton Distillery or the Leestown Distillery, its official title since 1969 is the Ancient Age Distillery or the Ancient Age Distilling Company.

ANCIENT AGE
AVAILABLE IN 40, 45, AND 50% ABV BOTTLINGS

RATING: 75

Old-fashioned style bourbon with a decent amount of oakiness in the nose and the familiar vanilla and honey notes peculiar to whiskey aged in new charred oak barrels.

The fairly light body presents a spicy, sharp, tangy palate, with some dry notes of tobacco. This would be a wonderful, if idiosyncratic, bottling if a sharp grassiness on the back of the palate didn't detract attention, however slightly, from the pleasing dryness.

Overall: A reasonably priced whiskey for mixed drinks or on the rocks as a light apéritif.

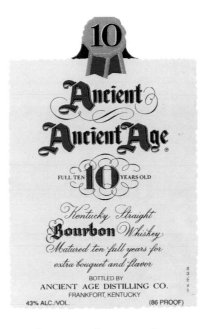

ANCIENT ANCIENT AGE
10 YEARS OLD, 43% ABV

RATING: 87

A gorgeous caramel nose with hints of vanilla, oranges, and a great herbal backdrop; the body is medium and very soft, and the palate presents some rich fruity notes, sweet vanilla, and a contrasting underlayer of fine old leather; the finish is medium-long and sweet.

Overall: A complex whiskey that's actually best over ice, but it's also a fine bourbon to sip neat.

Baker's Bourbon

DISTILLERY: The Jim Beam Distilleries, Clermont and Boston, Kentucky

THE WHISKEY: Baker's bourbon, named for retired distiller, Baker Beam, was introduced to the market in 1992. The label states that the whiskey ". . . follows our Beam family tradition of putting our best secrets inside the bottle, not here on the label" and recommends that it be savored "over ice," with a splash of water, or however you take your bourbon. For a complete history of the Beam family, see The Jim Beam Distillery (page 159).

53-1/2% ALC./VOL.
(107 PROOF)
KENTUCKY STRAIGHT BOURBON WHISKEY
(Aged in Wood)

BAKER'S

SEVEN YEARS OLD **107** PROOF 750ML

**BAKER'S BOURBON
7 YEARS OLD, 53.5% ABV**

RATING: 90

A sharp bourbon that displays a pleasing fruitiness in the nose and a medium body. The palate brings notes of nuts, vanilla, tobacco, and old leather; the finish is medium to long and ruggedly spicy.

Overall: A good gutsy bourbon, ideal on the rocks, or with water or club soda.

Barclay's Bourbon

Distillery: The Barton Distillery, Bardstown, Kentucky
The Whiskey: A brand name bought by this distillery some years ago—no one knows where the name came from. This bottling is primarily what restaurants term a "well," or generic, whiskey inasmuch as it is reasonably priced and not heavily promoted.

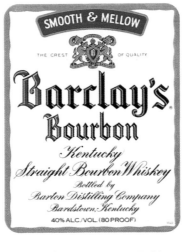

BARCLAY'S BOURBON, 40% ABV

RATING: 75

Oak and vanilla present in the nose; a light body with a simple, spicy palate, and an adequate but undistinctive finish.

Overall: This would be an ordinary whiskey if the distinctive spicy quality in the palate didn't come through so well. Save this one for mixed drinks.

Basil Hayden's Bourbon

DISTILLERY: The Jim Beam Distilleries, Clermont and Boston, Kentucky

THE WHISKEY: Named for an early Kentucky whiskey man, Basil Hayden is actually Old Grand-Dad himself, and you can read more about him on page 111. This bottling was introduced in 1992. Beam has done a good job to make the packaging of this bottling distinctive.

BASIL HAYDEN'S BOURBON, 8 YEARS OLD, 40% ABV

RATING: 88

A very spicy nose with notes of pepper balanced well with hints of citrus and mint; a lightish body and a very spicy palate that brings some fruits into play; the finish is of medium length, and like the rest of the whiskey, spicy and warming.

Overall: We can't help thinking that this whiskey would be better with an extra couple of years in the wood, but at eight years old, it should be fairly mature— maybe a higher proof would help here. Having said that, this whiskey is very stylistic, and if it's spice you're after, this one's for you. Sip it quickly on the rocks—you don't want to dilute it much more, but you might want to try keeping Basil Hayden's in the freezer and serving it neat before dinner.

Beam's Choice

DISTILLERY: The Jim Beam Distilleries, Clermont and Boston, Kentucky

THE WHISKEY: *See Jim Beam, page 91*

BEAM'S CHOICE, 40% ABV

RATING: 86

Oak and spices predominate in the nose; medium bodied with a fairly complex, spicy palate, complete with hints of moss; a medium-length finish that tingles in the throat.

Overall: A truly good bourbon, and not too pricey. Drink it on the rocks or with ginger ale.

Benchmark Bourbon

DISTILLERY: The Ancient Age Distillery, Frankfort, Kentucky

THE WHISKEY: Here's a whiskey that started out as one of Seagram's premium brands in 1967 and was sold to Sazerac, owner of The Ancient Age Distillery, in 1989. The single-barrel version—an export-only bottling—was first made available in 1995.

BENCHMARK
PREMIUM BOURBON®
SOUR MASH
KENTUCKY STRAIGHT BOURBON WHISKEY

BOTTLED BY THE OLD BENCHMARK COMPANY, NEW ORLEANS, LA
750 ml • ALC. 40% BY VOL. (80 PROOF)
44174-00

BENCHMARK PREMIUM BOURBON, 40% ABV
RATING: 85

A very sweet nose with lots of vanilla notes; light body and a smooth, sweet palate in which the vanilla predominates over an agreeably fruity backdrop; the whiskey falls down somewhat on the finish where a disagreeable touch of mint comes into play.

Overall: A fairly ordinary bourbon but if you like your whiskey sweet, this one's for you. Drink it on the rocks, or try it in a Manhattan.

KENTUCKY STRAIGHT BOURBON WHISKEY

BENCHMARK XO SINGLE-BARREL BOURBON, 47% ABV (FOR EXPORT ONLY)

RATING: 90

A complex nose with vanilla and oak balanced well with some floral notes; the body is full, and the palate, though similar to the nose, also bears a great spiciness and a hint of chocolate and/or caramel; the finish is medium and spicy.

Overall: A really good whiskey. Drink it neat or on the rocks.

Blanton's Single-Barrel Bourbon

DISTILLERY: The Ancient Age Distillery, Frankfort, Kentucky

THE WHISKEY: In 1984, this bottling became the first single-barrel bourbon on the market since Repeal. Well received by both the public and whiskey writers, the bottle comes complete with information on the singular whiskey inside—its barrel and bottle numbers, the warehouse, rick, and the bottling date.

This whiskey is named for the nineteenth-century master distiller at the Ancient Age Distillery, Albert B. Blanton. (You can read more about him on page 144.)

BLANTON'S SINGLE-BARREL BOURBON, 46.5% ABV (BOTTLE NO. 216, DUMPED ON 7/22/97 FROM BARREL NO. 1, STORED IN WAREHOUSE H ON RICK NO. 13)

RATING: 90

A sturdy nose showing tobacco, leather, and honey sitting atop a cushion of light spices; the body is medium but leans toward full, and the palate presents a good, yet simple balance of honey, vanilla, and tongue-tingling spices; the finish is medium.

Overall: A well-crafted bourbon that could use a little more complexity. Nevertheless, it's worthy of being sipped neat, on the rocks, or in a Manhattan.

Booker's Bourbon

Distillery: The Jim Beam Distilleries, Clermont and Boston, Kentucky

The Whiskey: Booker's Bourbon, named for Booker Noe, Jim Beam's grandson and Master Distiller Emeritus at the Jim Beam Distilleries, was released in 1989 and remains a sterling example of the whiskey-maker's craft. This is, at present, the only unfiltered bourbon on the market, and considering its popularity, we're surprised that more distilleries don't take note of that fact. Booker's bourbon is one of the few bourbons that is bottled at barrel proof (usually around 63% abv), and should your bottle get too cold, the whiskey might turn a bit cloudy. Worry not, that's the way unfiltered whiskey can react to cooler temperatures.

BOOKER'S BOURBON, UNFILTERED (BOTTLE No. 68458 SAMPLED FROM BATCH No. C-89-E-26, AGED 7 YEARS, 10 MONTHS, 62.8% ABV)

RATING: 96

A deep, rich nose with a complex mix of sweet vanilla, rich butter, oak, honey, caramel, leather, cloves, and a wonderful orangy backdrop; the body is huge, and the palate is very similar to the nose although it also presents some butterscotch notes, a larger dose of spices, and with a few drops of water, the orange flavors burst through along with some herbal qualities undetected when tasted neat; the finish is very long, rich, and spicy.

Overall: A classic bourbon. Cut it with about 25 percent spring water for post-prandial sipping, or drink it over lots of ice, or tall with lots of water.

Cabin Still Bourbon

DISTILLERY: The Heaven Hill Distillery, Bardstown, Kentucky

THE WHISKEY: This is a "well" bourbon.

CABIN STILL BOURBON, 40% ABV

RATING: 70

A flat, herbaceous nose with some oak notes; the body is thin, leaning toward watery, and the palate is flat and vegetal; the finish is hot.

Overall: If someone buys you this whiskey, and we hope they don't, reserve it for the kitchen.

Colonel Lee Bourbon

DISTILLERY: The Barton Distillery, Bardstown, Kentucky

THE WHISKEY: This is an inexpensive "well" bourbon with a colorful looking, yet completely fictitious character on the label.

COLONEL LEE, BOTTLED-IN-BOND, 50% ABV
RATING: 85

Fairly complex nose with the familiar vanilla springing over a fruity backdrop; a medium body, and a surprisingly complex palate showing a nice balance of oak, vanilla, and yet again, a somewhat deep fruity backdrop; the finish is fairly long and sweetish.

Overall: Good value for money here—we were astonished at the complexity of this whiskey. Oh, it's not the best of the best, but it's better than most of its ilk. Try Colonel Lee on the rocks or in mixed drinks.

Daniel Stewart Bourbon

DISTILLERY: The Heaven Hill Distillery, Bardstown, Kentucky

THE WHISKEY: This is a "well" bourbon that took its name from an old Kentucky inn sign.

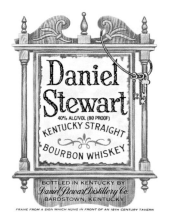

DANIEL STEWART BOURBON, 40% ABV

RATING: 70

A flat herbaceous nose with some oak notes; the body is thin, leaning toward watery, and the palate is flat and vegetal; the finish is hot.

Overall: Kitchen whiskey.

Eagle Rare Bourbon

DISTILLERY: The Ancient Age Distillery

THE WHISKEY: This is a bourbon that can't be found everywhere, but we urge readers to seek it out wherever they go. The brand name originated at Seagram's in the 1970s, and is said to have been introduced as direct competition to Wild Turkey—both sporting American birds as their motif. Eagle Rare is now produced at the Ancient Age Distillery, and the brand is owned by the Sazerac company of New Orleans.

EAGLE RARE BOURBON, 10 YEARS OLD, 50.5% ABV
RATING: 94

A sweet, oaky nose with an unusual herbaceous quality; the body is full, and the palate offers a complexity hard to find in most bourbons—deep fruits, a touch of honey, and even a touch of smokiness; the finish is extraordinarily long and very lush.

Overall: This bottling breaks all the rules for bourbon—it's almost reminiscent of a fine port wine. Serve this bourbon neat to guests who claim to dislike bourbon; you'll convert them. Drink it neat.

Early Times Bourbon

DISTILLERY: The Early Times Distillery, Louisville, Kentucky

Note: Early Times uses the Scottish spelling of whisky —without the *e*.

THE WHISKY: This brand of whisky originated at the Early Times Distillery close to Bardstown that was opened in 1860 by John H. Beam, uncle to Jim Beam. The whisky is currently made by Brown-Forman, who also make Old Forester, and is available in two styles—an "Old Style Kentucky Whisky" (partially aged in used cooperage), and two straight bourbons that are sold only in export markets. (Read about Early Times on page 151.)

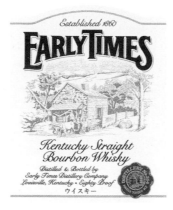

EARLY TIMES STRAIGHT BOURBON, 40% ABV, AND PREMIUM EARLY TIMES STRAIGHT BOURBON, 43% ABV (BOTH FOR EXPORT ONLY)

RATING: 86

A flowery nose with light vanilla notes and a hint of honey; medium body with more complexity than the nose suggests—although the predominant flavors are of tobacco and leather (with a pleasant backdrop of sweet vanilla). These bottlings have a lighter style than is usual in bourbons; the finish is warm and of medium length.

Overall: Early Times is an idiosyncratic bourbon with a somewhat old-fashioned quality and plenty of character. Drink it on the rocks or in mixed drinks.

Echo Springs Bourbon

Distillery: The Heaven Hill Distillery, Bardstown, Kentucky

The Whiskey: This is a "well" bourbon.

Echo Springs Bourbon, 40% abv

Rating: 70

A flat herbaceous nose with some oak notes; the body is thin, leaning toward watery, and the palate is flat and vegetal; the finish is hot.

Overall: Kitchen whiskey.

Elijah Craig Bourbon

DISTILLERY: The Heaven Hill Distillery, Bardstown, Kentucky

THE WHISKEY: This whiskey gets its name from an eighteenth-century Baptist minister who fled Virginia because of religious persecution at the hands of officials of the Church of England and settled in Kentucky where he preached—and made bourbon.

Craig was one of the first Kentucky whiskey makers to ship his product from Kentucky to New Orleans, and since the port most frequently used by Craig and other distillers was located in Bourbon County, it was these whiskeys that first became known as bourbon. After his death in 1808, Craig's obituary in the Kentucky Gazette declared, "If virtue consists of being useful to our fellow citizens, perhaps there are few more virtuous men than Mr. Craig."

ELIJAH CRAIG, 12 YEARS OLD, 47% ABV

RATING: 89

A delicate nose with vanilla, light fruits, and a hint of fresh mint; medium body with a palate much sweeter than the nose suggests, complete with oak notes, hints of dates, and a medium-long finish.

Overall: A well-crafted whiskey that's smooth enough and complex enough to sip neat, but also fares very well over ice.

Elijah Craig Single-Barrel Bourbon, 18 Years Old, 45% ABV, Barrel No. 209, Barreled on 12/14/78

Rating: 95

A buttery vanilla nose with some winey notes, a hint of caramel, and an aroma that can be described only as being reminiscent of Butterfingers candy bars; a medium body presents a dry, almost cognac-like palate with eucalyptus notes and some hints, in the backdrop, of deep rich caramel; the finish is crisp, dry, and lasts a lifetime.

Overall: Another single-barrel offering from Heaven Hill that has actually improved over the few years that it has been around, but the character seems to have changed completely. This used to be a fruity bottling, but the most recent example is more along the lines of a Delamain cognac—dry and austere. Sip it neat.

Elmer T. Lee Single-Barrel Bourbon

DISTILLERY: The Ancient Age Distillery, Frankfort, Kentucky

THE WHISKEY: This is a single-barrel bourbon, and as such, it's reasonable to expect slight differences from bottle to bottle. However, single-barrel whiskeys are always chosen to represent a particular style, so if you like one bottling, chances are, you'll also enjoy the next one. Elmer Tandy Lee is the twinkly-eyed Master Distiller Emeritus at this distillery, and he learned his craft from none other than Albert B. Blanton of Blanton's bourbon fame.

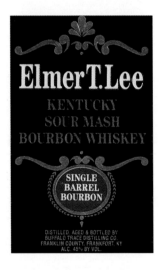

ELMER T. LEE SINGLE-BARREL BOURBON, 45% ABV
RATING: 91

A great nose that brings notes of butterscotch, clover, vanilla, and old leather; the body is big, and the palate bears an almost wine-like character that balances intense fruits, honey, and vanilla with a light spiciness that shows off the distiller's craft; the finish is long and warm.

Overall: A very well-crafted bourbon. Sip it neat, on the rocks, or in a Manhattan.

Evan Williams Bourbon

DISTILLERY: The Heaven Hill Distillery, Bardstown, Kentucky

THE WHISKEY: Evan Williams is well-known for being the first distiller to open a commercial distillery in Louisville in or around 1783. He was also a member of Louisville's Board of Trustees, and reportedly, Williams once brought a bottle of whiskey to one of the board's meetings where it was well received by the other members.

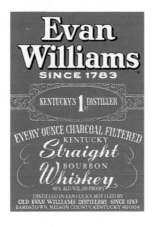

EVAN WILLIAMS, 40% ABV
RATING: 85

A lightish whiskey with a somewhat fragrant nose and slim body; the palate bears light notes of wildflowers, a pleasant oakiness, and has a sweetish herbaceous quality; the finish is short.

Overall: This is an apéritif-style bourbon, good for serving straight from the freezer before dinner. You can also use it successfully in mixed drinks.

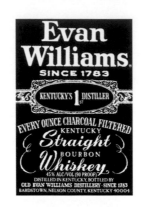

EVAN WILLIAMS, 7 YEARS OLD, 45% ABV

RATING: 87

A lightish nose with a waft of vanilla and a pleasant minty backdrop; the body is medium, though it leans toward being light, and the palate fares well in complexity showing delicate notes of oak, leather, and vanilla; the finish is medium.

Overall: This is a whiskey to serve on the rocks or in mixed drinks, providing you enjoy the fragrant style that the non-vintage Evan Williams bottlings offer.

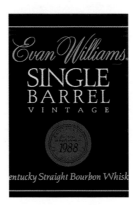

EVAN WILLIAMS SINGLE-BARREL BOURBON, VINTAGE 1988, 43.3% ABV

RATING: 90

A sweet, almost yeasty nose with notes of oak, caramel, spices, and a nice herbal backdrop; the medium body presents a vanilla sweetness followed by some wonderful herbaceous notes that are well balanced with traces of spice and menthol; the finish is both sweet and sharp.

Overall: A very well-crafted whiskey. Drink it neat or with a splash of spring water.

Evan Williams single-barrel Bourbon, Vintage 1989, 43.3% abv

Rating: 92

A nicely balanced nose with a complex mix of caramel, vanilla, herbs, and a very interesting mossy character; the body is medium, and the palate, although similar to the previous year's vintage bottling, presents an even better balancing act of the sweet vanilla notes playing as a cushion underneath the more prominent dry herbal qualities, and here we even detected a slight medicinal tang that was almost reminiscent of an Islay scotch. The finish is long, sharp, spicy, and dry.

Overall: A very well-crafted whiskey. Drink it neat or with a splash of spring water.

Ezra Brooks Bourbon

BOTTLER AND MARKETER: David Sherman Company, St. Louis, Missouri

DISTILLERY: Undisclosed

THE WHISKEY: Ezra Brooks bourbon was introduced in the mid-1950s when The Medley Distillery decided to compete with Jack Daniel's Tennessee whiskey by issuing a bottling with a similar label. Ezra Brooks is a fictitious name conjured up by marketers, but we must admit that he at least sounds as though he was an old Kentucky whiskey man.

EZRA BROOKS KENTUCKY STRAIGHT BOURBON, 45% ABV

RATING: 84

A honey-sweet nose with a simple herbaceous backdrop; medium body with a sweet, but not complex palate that brings some cocoa notes into play; the finish is medium.

Overall: A decent bottling though not complex enough to make it an after-dinner bottling. Drink it on the rocks or in mixed drinks.

Four Roses Bourbon

DISTILLERY: The Four Roses Distillery, Lawrenceburg, Kentucky

THE WHISKEY: You can read about the history of Four Roses on page 152. Here we should note that only one of these bottlings, the single-barrel bourbon, is currently available in the United States; look for the others in duty-free shops overseas. The Four Roses brand name is closely associated with their inexpensive blended whiskey in America, but these premium straight bourbons are in a category all their own.

FOUR ROSES BOURBON, 40% ABV (FOR EXPORT ONLY)

RATING: 87

A fragrant nose with hints of citrus and fresh herbs; medium body with a rich, oaky palate that displays some mild spices; the finish is of medium length and a little hot.

Overall: This is a well-crafted, fairly complex bourbon that can be sipped neat, on the rocks, or with water.

FOUR ROSES FINE OLD BOURBON, 40% ABV
(FOR EXPORT ONLY)

RATING: 89

A sweet-spicy nose with unmistakable clove notes; medium body with an interestingly complex palate that plays the toffeeish sweet notes off a tingly spiciness; the finish is fairly long and very smooth.

Overall: Another well-made bourbon from Four Roses —drink it neat, on the rocks, or in a Manhattan.

FOUR ROSES SUPER PREMIUM BOURBON,
43% ABV (FOR EXPORT ONLY)

RATING: 91

A sweet nose with the familiar clove notes present in the previous bottling; the body is a little bigger in this instance, and almost silky, bearing a palate that's very rich and sweet with honey notes, cocoa, intense vanilla, and a lush oakiness; the finish is long and very satisfying.

Overall: This bourbon fares very well when sipped neat at room temperature—the intense sweetness renders it a prime after-dinner bourbon. Cocktail fans are also advised to use this one to make superlative Manhattans.

FOUR ROSES SINGLE-BARREL RESERVE, 43% ABV, FROM BARREL NO. L70311

RATING: 96

A wonderfully balanced nose that shows sweet oak and caramel playing with soft spring flowers, a hint of fruit, and a dash of white pepper; the body is rich and full, and the palate is incredibly understated with a well-crafted balancing act—it bears the sweetness of dark chocolate (without any actual chocolate notes), the dryness of austere cognac, and a grand, yet mellow, bag of spices. The finish is long and dry.

Overall: A world-class whiskey. Drink it neat.

Gentleman Jack
Rare Tennessee Whiskey

DISTILLERY: The Jack Daniel Distillery, Lynchburg, Tennessee

THE WHISKEY: This super-premium bottling from the Jack Daniel Distillery was introduced to just ten markets in 1988 and then expanded nationwide just five years later. Gentleman Jack is different from regular Jack Daniel's Tennessee whiskeys in that it is filtered according to the Lincoln County process—through vats of sugar-maple charcoal—both before and after aging. Other Jack Daniel's bottlings are charcoal filtered just once, right before being put into barrels for maturation.

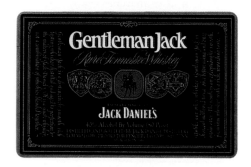

**GENTLEMAN JACK RARE TENNESSEE WHISKEY,
40% ABV**

RATING: 88

A honey-sweet nose with a dusty-sooty backdrop familiar to Tennessee whiskey drinkers; the big silken body brings a fruitier-than-most palate with a well-balanced and fairly complex mix of sharp, peppery spices; a long warm finish.

Overall: Although it's tempting to serve this whiskey neat, it fares much better over plenty of ice where its gutsiness reminds you that though this whiskey is more gentlemanly than its brothers, it's still a tough Tennessee whiskey.

George Dickel
Tennessee Sour Mash Whisky

Distillery: George A. Dickel's Cascade Distillery, Tullahoma, Tennessee

Note: Dickel spells whisky without the *e* usually used in American whiskeys.

The Whisky: Often known as Tennessee's other whisky, Dickel enjoys a great reputation in its home state and is made using the same Lincoln County Process that distinguishes Tennessee whiskeys from all others. This process, however, is somewhat different at the picturesque Dickel plant, inasmuch as the vats of sugar-maple charcoal are filled to the brim with new whisky, thus ensuring maximum contact with the charcoal, before being drained from the bottom into barrels for aging. (To find out more about George Dickel, see page 153.)

GEORGE DICKEL OLD No. 8 BRAND, 40% ABV

RATING: 86

A sweet, sooty nose with a refreshing touch of green apples; the medium body presents similar notes in the palate—apples and sweet Tennessee charcoal—but these are well-balanced with a backdrop of spices; the finish is medium in length and pleasantly warming.

Overall: This is what Tennessee whisky is all about. It's not a complex, refined drink to savor, but it has guts and gusto. Drink it from a shot glass or on the rocks.

GEORGE DICKEL No. 12 SUPERIOR BRAND, 45% ABV

RATING: 89

A similar nose to the No. 8 bottling, but with some honey notes adding to its complexity; a medium body and a palate that brings tobacco and leather into play; the finish is medium, pleasantly warm, and very sooty.

Overall: Although this bottling is more complex than Dickel's No. 8, we still suggest that you drink it from a shot glass or on the rocks—it's a quintessential Tennessee whisky.

GEORGE DICKEL SPECIAL BARREL RESERVE, 10 YEARS OLD, 43% ABV

RATING: 90

A thick, creamy nose that bears the telltale Tennessee sootiness but with the added nuance of caramel and old leather; a huge body and a complex palate complete with an abundance of spices and a backdrop of ripe fruits; a long, sophisticated, sooty finish completes the experience.

Overall: The finest Tennessee whiskey we've tasted. Sip it neat, late at night or whenever the yen for something rich and soothing grabs you.

Hancock's Reserve Single-Barrel Bourbon

DISTILLERY: The Ancient Age Distillery, Frankfort, Kentucky

THE WHISKEY: Hancock's Reserve is named for an early surveyor of Leestown, Hancock Taylor, and is just one of four single-barrel bourbons issued by this distillery.

HANCOCK'S RESERVE SINGLE-BARREL BOURBON, 44.45% ABV

RATING: 88

A light, sweet nose with traces of mango and papaya; the body is full, and the palate shows a nice, if simple, balance of honey, clover, a slight fruitiness, and a dash of spices; the finish is long and warm.

Overall: A well-crafted whiskey. Drink it on the rocks or in a Manhattan.

Heaven Hill Bourbon

DISTILLERY: The Heaven Hill Distillery, Bardstown, Kentucky

THE WHISKEY: *See Heaven Hill Distillery, page 155*

HEAVEN HILL, 40% ABV

RATING: 74

A light nose with subtle hints of wildflowers and honey; the body, too, is light, and the palate simple, a bit woody, and rather hot; the finish is medium-long and again, fairly hot.

Overall: Best reserved for mixed drinks.

HEAVEN HILL, 6 YEARS OLD, 40% ABV

RATING: 83

A perfumey nose with light vanilla notes; medium body and somewhat hot on the palate with notes of sweet honey, and surprisingly, a touch of supple leather; the finish is short to medium in length and pleasantly sweet.

Overall: A decent inexpensive bourbon suitable for drinking on the rocks or in mixed drinks.

Henry Clay Rare Bourbon

DISTILLERY: The Henry Clay Distillery, Kentucky

THE WHISKEY: This bourbon is one of the Rare American Whiskey collection being issued by The Classic Kentucky Bourbon Company, a subsidary of United Distillers, and may be hard to find. It comes from a very rare stock that was produced at a defunct Kentucky distillery that was opened by James E. Pepper in 1879. Check liquor stores for the odd bottle that might still be lurking on a shelf.

**HENRY CLAY RARE BOURBON,
16 YEARS OLD, 45.3% ABV**

RATING: 89

Lots of vanilla in the nose here, but there's also a touch of woodiness that detracts; the body is full and the palate, initially spicy, develops some fruit notes and even a hint of chocolate; the finish is long and spicy.

Overall: One of the few cases of very slightly overaged bourbons we've seen—this might have been great at, say, 14 years old. However, it has style all its own and should be sipped neat or with a drop of spring water.

Henry McKenna Bourbon

DISTILLERY: The Heaven Hill Distillery, Bardstown, Kentucky

THE WHISKEY: Henry McKenna, a nineteenth-century Irish immigrant, started making whiskey on his Kentucky farm around 1855 and was soon much more of a distiller than a farmer. His first whiskey, interestingly enough, was made from a wheat-based recipe, thus giving historical precedence to the wheated bourbons so popular today.

H. McKenna Old Line, Hand Made, Sour Mash Whisky had become very popular throughout the nation before McKenna died in 1893, and it was known for being of high quality since McKenna insisted on aging it properly before it was bottled.

Although McKenna's distillery was closed during Prohibition, his whiskey continued to be sold during the Noble Experiment—as medicinal stock. In 1934, McKenna's descendants reopened the plant and ran it until 1941, when it was sold to the Seagram company. The distillery closed in the mid-1970s, and the brand name is now owned by the Heaven Hill Distillery, which issues two bottlings—one great, the other not.

HENRY McKENNA, 40% ABV

RATING: 73

A light nose with hints of vanilla and an herbaceous backdrop; the medium body leans toward being light and the palate is bland bearing some oak notes mingled with a mintiness that, in this case, just doesn't work; the finish is medium.

Overall: An inexpensive bottling for use in mixed drinks.

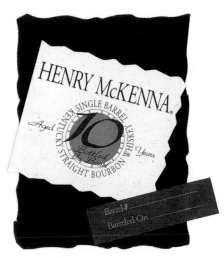

HENRY McKENNA 10-YEAR-OLD SINGLE-BARREL BOURBON, BARREL No. 087, BARRELED ON 12/5/86

RATING: 88

A good, traditional bourbon nose with a nice balance of vanilla, caramel, oak, and a light herbaceous note in the background; the body is medium, leaning toward full, and the palate shows a good balance of sharp spices, honey sweetness, and a touch of mint; the finish is very spicy.

Overall: This whiskey has improved since the first bottling, and according to Craig Beam, assistant distiller at this plant, it's because he is getting better at identifying which barrels to select for all their single-barrel bottlings. If you like your whiskey spicy, this one's for you. Drink it on the rocks.

I. W. Harper Bourbon

DISTILLERY: The Bernheim Distillery, Louisville, Kentucky

THE WHISKEY: This whiskey was first introduced by a company owned by Isaac Wolfe Bernheim, a German immigrant who entered the whiskey business in 1872 with his brother, Bernard, and a silent partner, Eldridge Palmer. It's said that he called the whiskey "Harper" because he needed an Anglo-Saxon name and Harper was the name of a friend who bred racehorses.

I. W. Harper bourbon won six gold medals between 1885 and 1915, and the 15-year-old I. W. Harper Gold Medal Bourbon, a relatively new bottling, also won a gold medal at the 1996 International Spirits Awards in London.

I. W. HARPER, 42% ABV
(A 50.5% ABV BOTTLING FOR EXPORT ONLY)

RATING: 87

A crisp, fragrant nose with hints of wildflowers and light fruits; the body is medium to full and the palate is extremely well-balanced with hints of fresh peaches mingling nicely with some sharp peppery spices; the finish falls halfway between medium and long.

Overall: A good apéritif whiskey suitable to being served chilled or on the rocks. We should mention, though, that the higher-proofed bottling is the more sophisticated of the two and offers a richer, more buttery palate that's just right for drinking neat.

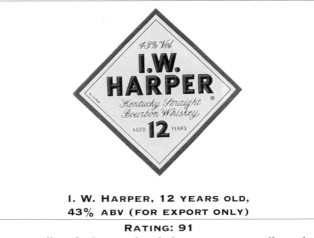

I. W. HARPER, 12 YEARS OLD, 43% ABV (FOR EXPORT ONLY)

RATING: 91

A well-crafted nose that balances sweet vanilla and a touch of honey with some fragrant spices; the medium body offers a very complex palate that plays a fruity sweet character off opposing notes of leather and spices with great skill; the finish is a little shorter than we expected, but has a very enjoyable spicy character.

Overall: Although this bourbon is certainly complex and smooth enough to be sipped neat, we much prefer it over ice.

I. W. HARPER GOLD MEDAL, 15 YEARS OLD, 40% ABV

RATING: 92

A rich, sweet nose with a wonderful backdrop of fine old leather; the full, rich, mouth-coating body presents an incredibly well-balanced palate that plays with your senses—it bears some fragrant wildflower notes, and then vanilla, leather, and oak come into play. Finally, there's a rich spiciness that tingles on the tongue; the finish is of medium length and very sharp and refreshing in the throat.

Overall: Once again, an extremely well-crafted whiskey that's very complex. We still prefer our I. W. Harper served over ice rather than sipped neat. This is proof, perhaps, that some great American whiskeys have been formulated to be served on the rocks.

I. W. HARPER PRESIDENT'S RESERVE, 43% ABV (FOR EXPORT ONLY)

RATING: 89

A fruity nose that gives way to a mellow spiciness; the medium body presents a spicy palate that gives way to an intense fruitiness—go figure—and brings some notes of leather into play; the finish is medium.

Overall: Here's the exception in the I. W. Harper line—this one fares better when served neat.

Jack Daniel's
Tennessee Sour Mash Whiskey

DISTILLERY: The Jack Daniel Distillery, Lynchburg, Tennessee

THE WHISKEY: Jack Daniel's Tennessee whiskey is probably the best-known whiskey in the world, and although many people mistake it for a bourbon, this is a true Tennessee whiskey—it goes through the Lincoln County Process, slowly drizzled over huge vats of sugar-maple charcoal before being aged.

There's more information about Jack Daniel on page 156, but travelers should note that if they visit this distillery, they should expect a great down-home-style tour complete with guides in overalls who sit and whittle as they wait for the next group of visitors to assemble. (And don't miss out on the family-style meals at Miss Mary Bobo's Boarding House in the town of Lynchburg [see page 167], where you're likely to be hosted by a Daniel family member.)

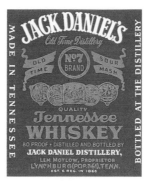

JACK DANIEL'S NO. 7 BRAND (GREEN LABEL), 40% ABV

RATING: 72

A light herbaceous nose with just a hint of sweetness; a thin body and a palate that reminds us more of the charcoal than the whiskey; the finish is short and hot.

Overall: If you want to use whiskey in the kitchen, this is the one.

JACK DANIEL'S OLD NO. 7 BRAND (BLACK LABEL), 43% ABV

RATING: 78

A sweetish nose with some pleasant tobacco notes; a light body that leans toward medium and a sooty palate that brings notes of light fruits that are almost, but not quite, overshadowed by a sharp pepperiness; the finish is medium and leaves a pleasant sooty trail in the throat.

Overall: Best described as a tough guy with a heart of gold, drink it straight or over lots of ice.

JACK DANIEL'S SINGLE-BARREL TENNESSEE WHISKEY, 47% ABV, DATE 1/29/97, BARREL NO. 7-1045, RICK NO. R13

RATING: 76

A rich, sweet nose with traces of mango, papaya, and a few herbal notes; the body is medium, leaning toward light, and the palate, though sooty as a Tennessee whiskey should be, is very simple with a few oaky vanilla notes and an almost astringent mouthfeel; the finish is short and sharp.

Overall: We prefer the Jack Daniel's Black label to this bottling, but it's interesting to taste another dimension of Tennessee whiskey. Drink it on the rocks.

Jacob's Well

DISTILLERY: The Jim Beam Distilleries, Clermont and Boston, Kentucky

THE WHISKEY: This whiskey is touted as being "twice-barreled," meaning that at a certain point in the aging process the master distiller mingles together maturing bourbon from specially selected barrels, and then returns the resultant mingling to the same barrels for further aging. A few blended scotches, such as Cutty Sark, also are aged in this way, and most distillers seem to agree that further aging after mingling gives whiskey a chance to develop more flavor.

JACOB'S WELL, 42% ABV, 84 MONTHS OLD

RATING: 84

The nose is light and fragrant but with a pleasant fruit-grain backdrop; the body is medium and the palate bears some honey-herbal notes along with a touch of sweet wood and a dash of spice; the finish is medium in length and carries a minty aftertaste.

Overall: We've had a hard time with this one—when it was first issued it seemed to be a pretty complex bottling, but more recent samplings have proved to be not quite as well constructed. Nonetheless, this fairly inexpensive bottling is pleasant and suitable for sipping on the rocks or in mixed drinks.

James E. Pepper Bourbon

DISTILLERY: The Bernheim Distillery, Louisville, Kentucky

THE WHISKEY: Released to foreign markets only, James E. Pepper bourbon is named for a member of one of Kentucky's earliest bourbon-making families. James's grandfather, Elijah Pepper, is said to have been making whiskey for sale as far back as 1780, and since he had been distilling for a few years at that time, his whiskey was once known as being "Born with the Republic." Elijah's son, Oscar, was the man who hired Dr. James Crow as his distiller (see page 160), and reputedly introduced the Old Fashioned cocktail to New York City.

JAMES E. PEPPER, 40% ABV (FOR EXPORT ONLY)

RATING: 74

A fragrant nose with a nice dose of sweet honey; the body is medium, and although the palate isn't very complex, it bears a nice balance of spices mingling with some smoky-leather notes; the finish is fairly short but contains a pleasant burst of spices.

Overall: Ideal for mixed drinks.

Jim Beam Bourbon

DISTILLERY: The Jim Beam Distilleries, Clermont and Boston, Kentucky

THE WHISKEY: After over 200 years in the whiskey business, the Beams know how to make and sell bourbon, and although the Beams don't actually own the distillery, the whiskey made there fairly shouts the Beam name. Shortly after Repeal, investors Harry Homel, Oliver Jacobson, and Harry Blum joined with Jim Beam, and his son, Jeremiah, to reopen what had been the Beam & Hart Distillery and resume production of the Beam's style of whiskey. Today, all the bourbons made there are still made under the close scrutiny of Master Distiller Emeritus, Booker Noe, grandson of Jim Beam, and a man who has bourbon in his blood.

JIM BEAM, 40% ABV

RATING: 84

Oaky-vanilla nose with a nice spicy backdrop; medium body, not too complex but the spices mingle well with vanilla on the palate; the short spicy finish is quite pleasant.

Overall: Reasonably priced, reasonably good whiskey; drink it on the rocks or in mixed drinks.

JIM BEAM BLACK, 7 YEARS OLD, 45% ABV

RATING: 94

A rich, deep nose with a complex mix of honey, butter, vanilla, caramel, prunes, and a straightforward dash of oak; the body wavers between being medium and full but leans toward the full side; the palate is incredibly well balanced bearing a vanilla richness together with fruit notes and a strong dash of old leather. The finish is long and lush.

Overall: Buy this bourbon. The black label Jim Beam used to be one year older than this bottling, but strange as it may sound, this one is even better than its older brother. Versatile to the max—drink it however you wish.

Joseph Finch Bourbon

DISTILLERY: The Finch Distillery, Pennsylvania (closed)
THE WHISKEY: This bourbon is one of the Rare American Whiskey Collection issued by The Classic Kentucky Bourbon Company and may be hard to find. It comes from a very rare stock that was made at a now closed Pennsylvania distillery, and once it's gone, it's gone. Check liquor stores for a bottle of this tasty whiskey.

JOSEPH FINCH RARE BOURBON, 15 YEARS OLD, 43.4% ABV

RATING: 92

A sweet, vanilla-caramel nose with nice touches of leather and tobacco in the background; the body is full and the palate bears a very nice balance of overripe fruits and spices; the finish is long and fairly heavy.

Overall: A really good dram that should be sipped neat.

J. T. S. Brown Bourbon

DISTILLERY: The Heaven Hill Distillery, Bardstown, Kentucky

THE WHISKEY: John Thompson Street Brown, the man for whom this whiskey is named, was half-brother to George Garvin Brown, the founder of the Brown-Forman company and originator of Old Forester bourbon. Although these men started out in business together in 1870, they soon parted ways and a whiskey company named J. T. S. Brown & Sons emerged in the early years of the twentieth century. This company eventually bought the Early Times Distillery, which, oddly enough, is now owned by Brown-Forman.

J. T. S. BROWN, 40% ABV

RATING: 73

A light, fragrant nose with just a touch of vanilla; the body is slim and the palate is somewhat minty with some undistinguished oak notes; the finish is very short.

Overall: An inexpensive bourbon for use only in mixed drinks.

J. W. Dant Bourbon

DISTILLERY: The Heaven Hill Distillery, Bardstown, Kentucky

THE WHISKEY: Joseph Washington Dant was a whiskey distiller in Kentucky back in 1836, and he's probably most famous for using a log as a still. This was an old-time method that was probably pretty common among settlers without enough money to buy a copper still, but Dant is the only man we know of who not only used a log still, but made whiskey good enough to ensure his name would survive the centuries.

J. W.'s son, George, opened a commercial distillery in 1870, and the J. W. Dant Company made whiskey until Prohibition, when production was stopped though existing stocks of Dant's bourbon were sold as medicinal whiskey. The brand name was eventually purchased by the Heaven Hill Distillery, present-day producers of J. W. Dant bourbon.

J. W. DANT, 40% ABV

RATING: 75

A very light, somewhat floral nose; slim body and a not too complex palate showing a touch of oak and a little too much mintiness; the finish is very short and fairly hot.

Overall: For use only in tall drinks with lots of mixer.

Kentucky Gentleman Bourbon

DISTILLERY: The Barton Distillery, Bardstown, Kentucky
THE WHISKEY: A "well" whiskey with no easily attainable history.

KENTUCKY GENTLEMAN, 6 YEARS OLD, 43% ABV
RATING: 75

A somewhat sweet nose with hints of tobacco; a medium body with a palate that is slightly sweet but with hints of spices; the finish is short and somewhat hot.

Overall: An inexpensive bourbon for use in mixed drinks.

Kentucky Tavern Bourbon Whiskey

Distillery: The Barton Distillery, Bardstown, Kentucky
The Whiskey: This label was first seen in the early years of this century when it was introduced as a blended whiskey. The name has changed hands a few times and was most recently purchased by the Barton Distillery. We are not sure whether the sample we tasted was actually made by this distillery or by the previous owners of the name.

Kentucky Tavern, 40% abv

Rating: 84

A sweet honeyed nose with a slightly spicy backdrop; the body is medium and the palate somewhat dry with leather coming into play and some lemon notes lurking in the background; the finish is medium.

Overall: A really decent inexpensive bottling suitable for mixed drinks, but also, strangely enough, quite obliging in a Manhattan cocktail.

Knob Creek Bourbon

DISTILLERY: The Jim Beam Distilleries, Clermont and Boston, Kentucky

THE WHISKEY: Knob Creek is the name of a small area near Bardstown, Kentucky, where Abraham Lincoln spent a few of his childhood years. During that time, Abe's father worked at a nearby distillery owned by Wattie Boone—a close relative of Daniel Boone, and one of the first commercial whiskey makers in the state.

Legend has it that Abe himself, although he would have been very young at the time, actually undertook some menial tasks at this plant, making the story somewhat plausible given that children of the time often worked in order to keep bread on the family table. But Abe wasn't too taken with whiskey. He grew up to be a temperance advocate, who promoted moderation rather than abstinence. It's said he once asked which whiskey General Grant drank so that he could send some to his other generals.

Knob Creek was introduced in 1992.

KNOB CREEK, 9 YEARS OLD, 50% ABV

RATING: 90

A heavy, sweet nose with an abundance of sweet grain and dark berries; the big body presents a palate that's very fruity but well-balanced with some oak-vanilla notes and a touch of caramelized sugar; the finish is long, and given the palate, surprisingly spicy.

Overall: Knob Creek is a very good bourbon that's very reasonably priced. We recommend you drink it on the rocks or in a Manhattan cocktail.

Maker's Mark Bourbon
(wheated)

DISTILLERY: The Maker's Mark Distillery, Loretto, Kentucky

Note: Maker's Mark spells whisky without the *e* usually used in American whiskeys.

THE WHISKY: Maker's Mark is made with wheat, rather than rye, as its secondary grain, and the recipe was developed by Bill Samuels Sr., with a little help from old-time whiskey man, Pappy Van Winkle (see Van Winkle Bourbon, page 127). You can read more about this whiskey, and the Samuels family, on page 161, but if you're planning a trip to bourbon country, you shouldn't miss visiting this exquisite distillery—it's a National Historic Landmark.

MAKER'S MARK, 45% ABV

RATING: 92

A rich, buttery nose with strong hints of raisins and honey; the big, soft body presents a complex, yet very easy palate with a veil of flavors that includes vanilla, honey, oranges, sweet butter, and a well-balanced backdrop of old leather with just a hint of spice; the finish is long, warm, and very smooth.

Overall: One of the most versatile whiskies on the market and reasonably priced at that. This one can be savored neat after dinner, in a great Manhattan, on the rocks, with a drop (but no more) of water, or even in mixed drinks.

MAKER'S MARK LIMITED EDITION, 50.5% ABV
(FOR EXPORT ONLY)
RATING: 93

A soft, sweet nose with a backdrop of cinnamon and cloves; the body is big, and the palate is spicier than the lower-proofed bottling with a great balance of cinnamon and nutmeg playing off some rich, buttery, vanilla notes; the finish is long and smooth.

Overall: This whisky is similar to the previous bottling, but perfect for anyone who likes more oomph. Serve this very versatile whisky however you please.

MAKER'S MARK SELECT, 47.5% ABV
(FOR EXPORT ONLY)
RATING: 95

A rich, sweet nose with notes of butter, vanilla, and raisins; the big body gives way to a very complex palate that seems to alternate between being buttery-sweet and herbaceously spicy with notes of fresh mint that complete the experience; the finish is long and warm, and once again, the fresh mint peeks through.

Overall: This whisky proves that Maker's Mark distillery can reach whatever heights it wishes. We rated the previous bottlings highly, but this one takes the cake. Drink it neat.

Mattingly & Moore Bourbon

DISTILLERY: The Heaven Hill Distillery, Bardstown, Kentucky

THE WHISKEY: This name dates back to the Mattingly and Moore Distillery which was opened in 1876 by Tom Moore and Ben Mattingly. A whiskey bearing the distillery name, however, didn't appear until 1896 after these two entrepreneurs had sold the plant. Tom Moore eventually opened the Tom Moore Distillery in Bardstown, on the site where the Barton Distillery now stands.

MATTINGLY & MOORE, 40% ABV

RATING: 85

A well-balanced nose with notes of sweet caramel, and nutty spices; the body is medium, and the palate shows a honeyed sweetness that counterpoints a minty character at the back of the throat; the finish is medium.

Overall: A good, reasonably priced bourbon that should be sipped over ice or in mixed drinks.

Old Charter Bourbon

DISTILLERY: The Bernheim Distillery, Louisville, Kentucky

THE WHISKEY: Old Charter was first produced by Adam and Ben Chapeze, descendants of a French surgeon who fought in the Revolutionary War. Their distillery was established by 1867, but the brand name was not created until 1874 when the Chapeze brothers decided to name it for the Charter Oak in Hartford, Connecticut, where the Governor's Charter was hidden from King James's soldiers in 1687.

Old Charter was not sold as medicinal stock during Prohibition, but the unsold, aging whiskey was stored at the Stitzel Distillery's warehouse. Just prior to Repeal, the brand was bought by the Bernheim Distillery, where it is still made today.

OLD CHARTER, 8 YEARS OLD, 40% ABV

RATING: 89

A complex, well-balanced nose that shows both dry, peppery notes, and a rich honey-vanilla sweetness; the body is medium, leaning toward full, and the palate follows the nose being at once dry and sophisticated with some tingly spicy notes, and also showing a sweet side full of toffee, vanilla, and a rich oakiness; the finish is very long and very satisfying.

Overall: This is a well-crafted bourbon with a balance that's hard to beat. Sip it neat, on the rocks, or in a Manhattan cocktail.

OLD CHARTER, 10 YEARS OLD, 43% ABV

RATING: 90

A similar nose to the previous bottling showing honeyed sweetness playing off some drier peppery notes, but this one also has a touch of old leather thrown in; the body is very big, and the palate is elegant and rich with the toffee sweetness playing off a potpourri of spices; the finish is long and smooth.

Overall: This great whiskey should be reserved for post-prandial consumption when it should be served neat (although it does work well over ice).

OLD CHARTER, THE CLASSIC 90,
12 YEARS OLD, 45% ABV

RATING: 92

The complex Old Charter nose is once again evident here, but this bottling is a little drier than the previous two; the body is big, and the palate, like the nose, is drier than the younger versions bringing a rich bunch of spices to the forefront and keeping the sweeter notes, now fruity rather than honeyed, as a backdrop; the finish is long and spicy.

Overall: Another great whiskey from Old Charter—sip it neat or on the rocks.

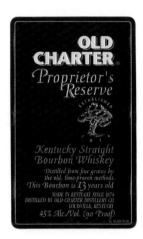

OLD CHARTER PROPRIETOR'S RESERVE, 13 YEARS OLD, 45% ABV

RATING: 98

The dry-sweet balance in the Old Charter bottlings are mingled together so well in this one that it's hard to know what's coming next. In the nose it's the dry pepperiness that hits first, but it's followed swiftly by a rich, sweet buttery note; the body is huge and creamy, coating your whole mouth, and the palate brings old leather into play with an abundance of fruits, cloves, and sweet vanilla; the finish is long and very sophisticated.

Overall: A classic world-class whiskey. Drink it neat.

Old Crow Bourbon

DISTILLERY: The Jim Beam Distilleries, Clermont and Boston, Kentucky

THE WHISKEY: This brand name dates back to 1823 when Dr. James Crow, a Scottish immigrant who was reputedly a chemist and physician, became a master distiller in Kentucky and revolutionized the whiskey business.

Crow utilized litmus paper, a saccharometer, and a thermometer, to make his whiskey. He not only perfected the sour-mash method, he aged his bourbon well before the practice was a norm in the industry. In our opinion, James Crow invented bourbon as we know it.

Crow developed his formula at the Old Oscar Pepper Distillery, a plant now reopened as the Labrot & Graham Distillery (page 160). Old Crow is now produced by the Jim Beam Brands Company, which reputedly uses a heavy hand when adding sour mash to its fermenters. We think Jim Crow would approve.

OLD CROW, 40% ABV

RATING: 81

A strong tobacco nose with a faint fruity-sweet backdrop; the body is medium leaning toward light, and the palate is somewhat fragrant with citrus notes balancing well with a light spiciness; the finish is short.

Overall: A really decent inexpensive whiskey. If you enjoy a sharp, peppery bourbon rather than a sweeter, more honeyed bottling, drink this one on the rocks, otherwise it's a good choice for mixed drinks.

Old Ezra Rare Old Sippin' Whiskey

BOTTLER AND MARKETER: The David Sherman Company, St. Louis, Missouri
DISTILLERY: Undisclosed
THE WHISKEY: *See Ezra Brooks, page 72*

OLD EZRA RARE OLD SIPPIN' WHISKEY, 7 YEARS OLD, 50.5% ABV

RATING: 89

A sweet nose with a wonderful backdrop of old leather; medium body with a palate bearing notes of sweet butter, rich vanilla, and chocolate; a long finish with an interesting clover note.

Overall: This is a well-crafted whiskey that can be served neat, on the rocks, or in a Manhattan.

Old Fitzgerald Bourbon
(wheated)

DISTILLERY: The Bernheim Distillery, Louisville, Kentucky

THE WHISKEY: Old Fitzgerald started its life in 1870 when John E. Fitzgerald opened a distillery in Frankfort, Kentucky, and produced a bourbon that he made available only to private clubs and luxury steamships.

In around 1900 he broadened his market when he released his brand to the American public at large and also to bourbon lovers in Europe. Old Fitzgerald remained one of the few bourbons made entirely in pot stills right up until 1913. The Old Fitzgerald brand was bought during Prohibition by Pappy Van Winkle (see page 114), a revered whiskey man who had been in the business since the late 1800s, and it became his favorite brand. Van Winkle was known to love wheated whiskeys, and not only is the brand now bearing his name made with a touch of wheat, Pappy also had a hand in developing Maker's Mark wheated bourbon.

OLD FITZGERALD PRIME BOURBON, 40% ABV, AND OLD FITZGERALD BOTTLED-IN-BOND BOURBON, 50% ABV

RATING: 87

A fragrant nose with light citrus playing off sweeter honeyed tones; the body is medium, and the palate rich with leather, spices, and a sweeter backdrop of vanilla, which is more pronounced in the higher-proof bottling; the finish is medium.

Overall: A good, very well-balanced bourbon suitable for drinking on the rocks or in mixed drinks.

OLD FITZGERALD 1849 BOURBON, 8 YEARS OLD, 45% ABV

RATING: 88

A rich, buttery nose with leather and vanilla playing off some lighter herbaceous notes; the body is big and supple and the palate fairly fruity with a good balance of spices and tobacco thrown in; the finish is very long.

Overall: This is a very good bottling, we recommend you drink it neat.

Old Forester Bourbon

DISTILLERY: The Early Times Distillery, Louisville, Kentucky

THE WHISKEY: Old Forester was first introduced around 1870 when George Garvin Brown, founder of the Brown-Forman beverage company, became the first to sell bourbon exclusively in sealed bottles. Prior to this revolutionary step, unscrupulous retailers often filled empty bottles that bore a reputable whiskey-maker's name with an inferior product they had purchased by the barrel or jug. George Garvin Brown wanted consumers to know exactly what they were buying, namely, his whiskey, Old Forester.

Note: We have chosen to review these two bottlings, differing only by proof, separately, because the bottled-in-bond whiskey is so different from the lower-proofed bourbon.

OLD FORESTER, 43% ABV
RATING: 87

A spicy nose with some sweet vanilla peeking through; the body is medium, and the palate, once again, predominantly spicy, but with a somewhat sweeter backdrop with hints of caramelized oranges and a whisper of vanilla; the finish is medium and nicely spiced.

Overall: This bourbon is incredibly well crafted considering its reasonable price, and should be considered a great whiskey to drink on the rocks.

OLD FORESTER, BONDED, 50% ABV

RATING: 91

A wonderfully complex nose with a host of spices, and a hint of both maple syrup and old leather to complete the experience; the body is full and the palate offers an initial burst of vanilla sweetness followed closely by some rich fruity notes, a smattering of supple old leather, and a host of peppery spices.

Overall: We have always liked this bottling. When we tasted this blind, we thought we were sampling a very expensive boutique bottling. Sip this one neat, on the rocks, or in a wonderfully spicy Manhattan.

Old Grand-Dad Bourbon

DISTILLERY: The Jim Beam Distilleries, Clermont and Boston, Kentucky

THE WHISKEY: The name on this label, Old Grand-Dad, refers to eighteenth-century whiskey distiller, Basil Hayden, whose grandson, Raymond B. Hayden, named a bourbon for his forefather in the mid-1800s. The Wathen family, who can also trace their whiskey-making heritage back to the late 1700s, eventually took over this brand, and although the original Old Grand-Dad Distillery was closed during Prohibition, the whiskey was still available by prescription throughout the Noble Experiment, and Old Grand-Dad was back on the open market shortly after Repeal. It's said that this whiskey is still made to the original nineteenth-century formula, and we have been told that there is much more rye used in this whiskey than in any other bourbon available today.

OLD GRAND-DAD, 43% ABV

RATING: 86

A spicy nose with hints of dried fruits; a medium body and a palate that shows some sweet vanilla, but more evident is the peppery spiciness displayed by notes of cloves and cinnamon; the finish is long and very spicy.

Overall: A very stylish whiskey with great complexity. It's best sipped over ice.

OLD GRAND-DAD BOTTLED-IN-BOND, 50% ABV
RATING: 87

The spicy nose displays some supple leather notes and just a trace of honey sweetness; the medium body leans a little on the full side, and the palate shows great balance with cinnamon and cloves, playing nicely off old leather and tobacco; the finish is long and spicy.

Overall: Drink it on the rocks.

OLD GRAND-DAD 114 BARREL PROOF, 57% ABV
RATING: 91

The nose is somewhat fragrant but also bears a complex gathering of vanilla, leather, and tobacco; the body is big, and the palate spicy with a conglomeration of sweet oak, rich vanilla, and dried fruits serving as a lush backdrop for the predominantly clove and cinnamon front notes; the finish is very long and luxurious.

Overall: A totally well-crafted bourbon. Drink it with a drop of bottled water or on the rocks.

Old Heaven Hill Bourbon

Distillery: The Heaven Hill Distillery, Bardstown, Kentucky

The Whiskey: *See Heaven Hill Distillery, page 155*

Old Heaven Hill, 10 years old, 43% abv
Rating: 88

A sweetish nose with a pleasant oaky-vanilla component; the medium body leans toward being big but doesn't quite make it, and the palate, bearing some familiar vanilla and oak notes also brings hints of dark cocoa and rich fruits; the finish is fairly long.

Overall: This bottling has improved since we last sampled it and is now suitable for sipping neat. However, it fares better over lots of ice and makes a really good Manhattan.

Old Rip Van Winkle Bourbon
(wheated)

BOTTLER AND PRODUCER: The Old Rip Van Winkle Distillery, Kentucky

THE WHISKEY: This company is headed by Julian Van Winkle, grandson of Pappy Van Winkle, a man mentioned often in this book and in Kentucky's whiskey industry as a whole. As far back as 1893, Pappy was a whiskey salesman who had a reputation as a wonderfully skilled raconteur and as a man who actually sold whiskey to moonshiners who added it to their white lightning to make it saleable. These bottlings are made, as Pappy would have liked it, with a touch of wheat in the recipe as opposed to the rye grain that's preferred by many distillers, and the first Van Winkle bottling was made available before Prohibition.

Asleep Many Years in the Wood

Old RIP VAN WINKLE
ALC. 45%/VOL. (90 PROOF)

Handmade Bourbon
Kentucky Straight Bourbon Whiskey
Genuine Old Line Sour Mash
From Old Rip Van Winkle Distillery

**OLD RIP VAN WINKLE BOURBON,
10 SUMMERS OLD, 45% ABV**

RATING: 91

A rich vanilla nose with a healthy dose of nutmeg, cloves, and a fruity backdrop; the body is big and the palate starts with a faint mossiness that quickly gives way to a complex mélange of spiced fruits; the finish is long and very spicy.

Overall: A high-quality bourbon that would be near perfect if it weren't for the initial swift mossy note in the palate. However, we could be being picky here, and that often happens when a whiskey is so well-crafted. Sip it neat or with a few drops of spring water, or drink it on the rocks.

OLD RIP VAN WINKLE BOURBON, 15 YEARS OLD, 53.5% ABV

RATING: 98

The nose bears rich butter, maple syrup, brown sugar, and a thin veil of nutmeg as a backdrop; the body is huge, and the palate is extremely well-balanced playing around with your senses as it presents sweet butter, dark fruits, leather, and tobacco intermingling with a host of tongue-tickling spices; the finish is long, and as the sweetness stays in the throat, the spices linger in the mouth.

Overall: A classic whiskey. Drink it neat.

Old Taylor Bourbon

DISTILLERY: The Jim Beam Distilleries, Clermont and Boston, Kentucky

THE WHISKEY: Colonel Edmund Haynes Taylor Jr. was one of the most respected men in the bourbon business, and although he started his distilling career around 1870, it wasn't until seventeen years later that he introduced Old Taylor bourbon to the marketplace. Taylor probably is best remembered for the part he played in ensuring that the Bottled-in-Bond Act was passed in 1897, and this act made sure that consumers could rely on the fact that whiskey bearing the governmental bottled-in-bond designation was straight whiskey and at least of four years old.

OLD TAYLOR, 6 YEARS OLD, 40% ABV

RATING: 86

A spicy nose with a gentle vanilla backdrop; the medium body bears a palate that's well-balanced between a clove spiciness and a vanilla sweetness; the finish is medium, verging on long, and fairly spicy.

Overall: A reasonably priced bourbon that has a lot going for it, but doesn't quite make it as a whiskey worth sipping neat. Drink this one over ice or in mixed drinks.

Old Weller Antique
The Original 107 Brand Bourbon
(wheated)

DISTILLERY: The Bernheim Distillery, Louisville, Kentucky

THE WHISKEY: *See W. L. Weller Bourbon, page 138.*

OLD WELLER ANTIQUE, THE ORIGINAL 107 BRAND BOURBON, 7 SUMMERS OLD, 53.5% ABV

RATING: 90

A sweetish nose with some unusual floral notes and a strong dash of vanilla; the body is big and the palate is very well-balanced, flirting with sweet honeyed fruit notes, a strong vanilla undertone, and some sharp spicy tones; the finish is long and spicy.

Overall: Another well-crafted whiskey from Weller. Sip it at room temperature with a few drops of spring water, or over ice.

Pappy Van Winkle Family Reserve Bourbon
(wheated)

BOTTLER AND PRODUCER: The Old Rip Van Winkle Distillery, Kentucky

THE WHISKEY: *See Old Rip Van Winkle, page 114*

Bottled by Old Rip Van Winkle Distillery • Lawrenceburg, Kentucky

PAPPY VAN WINKLE FAMILY RESERVE KENTUCKY STRAIGHT BOURBON, 20 YEARS OLD, 45.2 ABV

RATING: 98

The nose is intensely fruited but also bears a tantalizing citrus zest note; the body is huge and almost chewable, and the palate is tremendously buttery with some sherry notes, a dash of dried fruits, and some rich, creamy vanilla; the finish is long and elegant.

Overall: Drink this one neat—it's a classic example of what extra time in the wood can accomplish despite what some distillers may tell you about American whiskey getting too woody after half a dozen years. One of the world's finest whiskeys.

President's Choice Bourbon

DISTILLERY: The Labrot & Graham Distillery, Versailles, Kentucky

THE WHISKEY: Not available in the United States, this whiskey is issued by the Labrot & Graham Distillery, but since their operations didn't begin until 1996, the whiskey itself comes from specially selected barrels owned by Brown-Forman, the parent company.

PRESIDENT'S CHOICE BOURBON, 50.2% ABV (FOR EXPORT ONLY)

RATING: 89

A fruity nose with hints of oranges and mangos laced with sweet butter and a touch of spice; the body is medium but leans toward being full, and the palate is velvety rich with a nice balance of butter, vanilla, caramel, and a light spicy backdrop; the finish is long, smooth, and spicy.

Overall: Sip it neat, in a great Manhattan, or on the rocks; this is good whiskey.

Rebel Yell Bourbon
(wheated)

DISTILLERY: The Bernheim Distillery, Louisville, Kentucky

THE WHISKEY: Held in high regard in the southern United States, and not too well-known up north, this whiskey is actually a different bottling of W. L. Weller bourbon. The brainchild of Charlie Farnsley, Mayor of Louisville from 1948 until 1953, it was his idea to market a bourbon specifically to Southerners, and when it was first released in 1936, it couldn't be found north of the Mason-Dixon line. Now, Rebel Yell, a wheated bourbon, is available nationwide.

REBEL YELL, 40% ABV
RATING: 90

A soft, honeyed nose with a hint of lush dried fruits; the body leans toward being huge, and the palate is buttery rich with a pleasant balance of sweet fruits and just a hint of spice; the finish is medium.

Overall: A really good, well-priced whiskey that should be sipped straight, over ice, or in a Manhattan.

Rock Hill Farms Single-Barrel Bourbon

DISTILLERY: The Ancient Age Distillery, Frankfort, Kentucky

THE WHISKEY: Rock Hill Farms bourbon is named for the farm that used to stand on the site of the Ancient Age Distillery. It is a single-barrel offering, and as such, can differ slightly from one bottle to the next; however, single-barrel bourbons are always chosen with a particular flavor profile in mind, so if you enjoy one bottling of this whiskey, chances are that you'll enjoy the next.

ROCK HILL FARMS SINGLE-BARREL BOURBON, BOTTLED IN BOND, 50% ABV

RATING: 85

The nose presents hints of plums, candy, and papaya; and, the medium body bears a simple palate with a touch of fruit and tobacco, and a pleasant minty backdrop; the finish is medium.

Overall: Sad to say that this bottling isn't as good as it used to be, but it's still a good, if not too complex, rendition. Drink it on the rocks.

Stitzel-Weller Rare Bourbon
(wheated)

DISTILLERY: The Stitzel-Weller Distillery, Shively, Kentucky (closed)

THE WHISKEY: You can read more about the Weller family under W. L. Weller Bourbon, page 138. This whiskey was made at the old Stitzel-Weller Distillery, which opened on Kentucky Derby Day in 1935 and, sad for bourbon lovers, closed its doors in 1992. This bottling is one of the Rare American Whiskey Collection issued by The Classic Kentucky Bourbon Company. It comes from a very limited stock of whiskey distilled in 1980 and provides us the last-ever chance to sample bourbon made at this now-defunct plant.

At the time of publication, it's unclear when or if this bottling will be released

STITZEL-WELLER BOURBON, 17 YEARS OLD, 53.5% ABV—BARREL SAMPLE (FOR EXPORT ONLY)
RATING: 98

A sweet caramel nose with a touch of licorice and a delightful hint of mint; the body is huge, almost chewy, and intensely creamy, and the palate starts off with an immense vanilla sweetness that develops into notes of butterscotch, a hint of clover, and then a burst of tongue-tingling black pepper; although this whiskey seems to disappear in the throat, it has an uncanny ability to return after a couple of seconds leaving a rich sweetness for a long time.

Overall: A world-class whiskey, we advise that you add just a couple of drops of spring water and then sip it after dinner.

Ten High Bourbon

Distillery: The Barton Distillery, Bardstown, Kentucky
The Whiskey: An inexpensive "well" bourbon with no readily available history.

Ten High, 40% abv

Rating: 82

A sweetish vanilla nose with a hint of spice; the body is medium but leans toward light, and the palate, though simple, offers a good balance of toffee and vanilla with, yet again, a spicy undertone; the finish is short.

Overall: A really decent inexpensive bourbon ideal for cocktails and mixed drinks.

Tom Moore Bourbon

DISTILLERY: The Barton Distillery, Bardstown, Kentucky
THE WHISKEY: This brand name was first released in 1879 and refers to nineteenth-century distiller, Thomas Moore, who founded a distillery on the site where the present-day Barton Distillery now stands. The limestone-filtered water, emanating from a small spring that probably caused Moore to choose this particular site for his distillery, is still used to produce all the whiskey made at the Barton plant, but it is now supplemented by water from a nearby spring-fed lake. You can read more about Thomas Moore on page 147.

TOM MOORE, 40% ABV
RATING: 73

A light, fragrant nose and light body with a simple palate that offers some fruit notes and a touch of honey that is almost masked by a mintiness that is somewhat disagreeable; the finish is short.

Overall: A simple bourbon without a great deal of character, use it in mixed drinks.

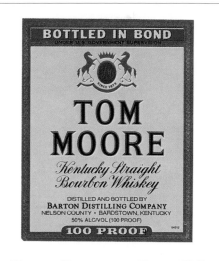

TOM MOORE, BOTTLED IN BOND, 50% ABV

RATING: 76

A sweetish nose with a touch of caramel; the body is light, but the palate has character that's displayed in a good balancing of spices, citrus zest, and a touch of honey; the finish is medium.

Overall: This is a decent inexpensive bourbon for use in mixed drinks; it even can be served successfully over ice.

T. W. Samuels Bourbon

DISTILLERY: The Heaven Hill Distillery, Bardstown, Kentucky

THE WHISKEY: This is a "well" bourbon that takes its name from the Samuels family of Maker's Mark fame. We presume that when the Samuels family decided to call their whiskey Maker's Mark, they simply sold off the rights to this label.

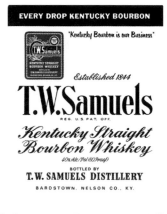

T. W. SAMUELS BOURBON, 40% ABV

RATING: 70

A flat herbaceous nose with some oak notes; the body is thin, leaning toward watery, and the palate is flat and vegetal; the finish is hot.

Overall: Kitchen whiskey.

Van Winkle Special Reserve Bourbon
(wheated)

BOTTLER AND PRODUCER: The Old Rip Van Winkle Distillery, Kentucky

THE WHISKEY: *See Old Rip Van Winkle, page 114*

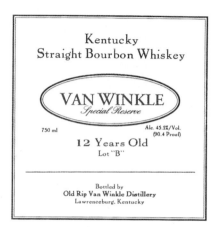

Kentucky
Straight Bourbon Whiskey

VAN WINKLE
Special Reserve

750 ml   Alc. 45.2%/Vol.
(90.4 Proof)

12 Years Old
Lot "B"

Bottled by
Old Rip Van Winkle Distillery
Lawrenceburg, Kentucky

**VAN WINKLE SPECIAL RESERVE KENTUCKY
STRAIGHT BOURBON, 12 YEARS OLD, 45.2% ABV**

RATING: 90

A sweet, toffeeish nose with a pleasantly fruity backdrop; a big body with an almost sherried palate that leans toward dried fruits with a subdued spiciness; the finish is long and spicy.

Overall: A very good bourbon. Drink it neat or on the rocks.

Very Old Barton Bourbon

DISTILLERY: The Barton Distillery, Bardstown, Kentucky

THE WHISKEY: Generally regarded as a "well" bourbon, the 6-year-old bottlings offer more than most whiskeys in this category. The name, Barton, comes from the distillery, but no one knows why the distillery is called Barton.

VERY OLD BARTON BOTTLED IN BOND, 50% ABV

RATING: 78

The nose offers oak and vanilla, but no real complexity; the body is medium with a hot, oaky palate and a hot, oaky finish.

Overall: A decent bourbon to drink over ice with mixers added.

**VERY OLD BARTON, 6 YEARS OLD,
AVAILABLE IN 40, 43, AND 45% ABV BOTTLINGS**

RATING: 82

Spicy nose with light fruit notes; a lightish body with a somewhat complex spicy-fruity-toffee palate that also bears a slight hint of leather. The whiskey, unfortunately falls down on the finish which is very short, but does have an interesting spicy quality.

Overall: Good value for the money in these bottlings; drink them on the rocks, or in mixed drinks.

Very Special Old Fitzgerald
(wheated)

DISTILLERY: The Bernheim Distillery, Louisville, Kentucky

THE WHISKEY: *See Old Fitzgerald, page 107*

VERY SPECIAL OLD FITZGERALD, 12 YEARS OLD, 45% ABV

RATING: 96

An enormously complex nose showing sweet vanilla, rich leather, and a berry-fruitiness; the body is huge and the palate is even more complex than the nose—honey, sweet butter, and dark berries playing well off the leather notes, and a hint of tobacco; the finish is extremely long.

Overall: A connoisseur's bourbon. Drink it neat or with a splash of water, or if you want a great Manhattan, spoil yourself with this bottling.

Virginia Gentleman Bourbon

DISTILLERY: A. Smith Bowman Distillery, Fredericksburg, Virginia

THE WHISKEY: This is the only bourbon matured in the state of Virginia. It was introduced in 1937 and is now a favorite among many power brokers in the nation's capital. You can read more about Virginia Gentleman Bourbon on page 146.

Note: This whiskey is now also available in a 45% abv bottling that we were unable to obtain for tasting.

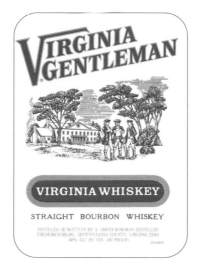

VIRGINIA GENTLEMAN BOURBON, 40% ABV
RATING: 85

A light floral nose with a dash of honeyed vanilla and a high note of fresh mint; the body is medium, leaning toward light, and the palate is very soft with notes of sweet vanilla, light oak, and a subtle dash of spices; the finish is medium.

Overall: An apéritif-style bourbon suitable for serving chilled, before dinner. People who like their whiskey on the light side might also choose to sip this one on the rocks.

Walker's DeLuxe Bourbon

PRODUCER: Hiram Walker & Sons, Inc., Detroit, Michigan

THE WHISKEY: This is an inexpensive bottling of "well" bourbon that was introduced in the 1940s.

WALKER'S DeLuxe STRAIGHT BOURBON, 40% ABV

RATING: 96

A fragrant nose with some toffee undertones; the body is light and the palate bears a floral character with a touch of caramel; the finish is short.

Overall: An inexpensive whiskey for use in tall mixed drinks.

Wathen's Kentucky Bourbon

DISTILLERY: The Charles Medley Distillery, Owensboro, Kentucky

THE WHISKEY: You can read more about the Wathen-Medley family on page 150, but this whiskey, released in 1996, is a product that comes from the eighth generation of a great Kentucky distilling dynasty. Although this claim doesn't appear on the label, Wathen's is a single-barrel bourbon.

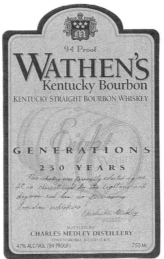

WATHEN'S KENTUCKY BOURBON, 47% ABV, BARREL NO. 10, HAND BOTTLED ON 3/27/97

RATING: 92

The nose is sharp, dry, and flowery, but has a wonderful underlay of sweet vanilla; the body is medium to full and buttery rich, and the palate is complex with notes of butterscotch, caramel, and a dense blanket of spices; the finish is long, dry, spicy, and sophisticated.

Overall: We are not of the school that believes bourbon suffers after too long in the wood, but here's a bottling with no age statement (denoting a minimum of only four years old) that bears all the sophistication of a decade-old whiskey. Sip it neat or on the rocks.

Wild Turkey Bourbon

DISTILLERY: The Wild Turkey Distillery, Lawrenceburg, Kentucky

THE WHISKEY: Wild Turkey is known throughout the world, and it got its name when Thomas McCarthy, then president of Austin, Nichols & Company, Inc., took a bottle of his company's bourbon on a wild turkey shoot in the 1940s. You can read more about Wild Turkey on page 163 but we would like to mention right here that, to our knowledge, not one distiller in the whole of Kentucky ever has a bad word to say about this wonderful whiskey.

WILD TURKEY, 40% ABV

RATING: 90

A very direct nose that brings thick notes of sweet vanilla intermingled with deep orange flavors; the big body presents some distinctive spice notes that are nicely balanced with a backdrop of ripe oranges; the finish is long and spicy.

Overall: Although not overly complex, this is an amazingly well-balanced bottling with lots of gutsy flavor. Drink it on the rocks or in a Manhattan.

WILD TURKEY OLD NUMBER 8 BRAND, 50.5% ABV
RATING: 92

A complex nose bearing notes of white pepper, lush fruits, and tobacco; the huge body brings a bold palate full of a very complex gathering of honey, fruits, and vanilla mingling with the spicier notes of nutmeg, cinnamon, cloves, and tobacco; the finish is long and once again, very complex with spices and fruits playing off one another.

Overall: A great bottling for all who like full-flavored whiskeys with deep complexity and soul. Sip it neat or on the rocks.

WILD TURKEY, 12 YEARS OLD, 50.5% ABV
RATING: 94

A wine-like nose with a faint but glorious floral backdrop; the body is huge and the palate much fruitier than the previous Wild Turkey bottlings with sweet berries, oranges, and rich vanilla notes predominating; the finish is long and nutty.

Overall: An idiosyncratic bourbon—very complex, and great to serve to people who think they don't like whiskey. This one proves that American whiskeys, when well-crafted, can come in many styles. Drink it neat.

WILD TURKEY RARE BREED, BARREL PROOF AT 54.4%, BATCH NO. W-T-01-96, BOTTLED AT 11:32 A.M. ON 11/20/96

RATING: 96

A round, rich nose with hints of wildflowers, caramel, oak, tobacco, and leather; the body is thick and syrupy and the palate is buttery sweet with touches of honey and the same leather/tobacco notes found in the nose, but then a burst of spices come through and make this whiskey incredibly complex; the finish is long, luxurious, and spicy.

Overall: A world-class whiskey. Sip it neat, on the rocks, or with just a drop of spring water.

WILD TURKEY KENTUCKY SPIRIT, SINGLE-BARREL BOURBON, 50.5% ABV, BOTTLED ON 11/9/96 FROM BARREL NO. 3 STORED IN WAREHOUSE B ON RICK NO. 13

RATING: 98

A sturdy tobacco nose with lots of honey, leather, caramel, and an interesting mossy note; the body is full, and the palate offers similar notes as the nose, but now there's also an incredible spiciness that intermingles with the other flavors admirably and presents an experience that's akin to tasting a very old cognac; the finish is extremely long and spicy warm.

Overall: A first-class, world-class bourbon. Sip it neat or on the rocks.

W. L. Weller Bourbon
(wheated)

DISTILLERY: The Bernheim Distillery, Louisville, Kentucky

THE WHISKEY: William LaRue Weller, a descendant of eighteenth-century whiskey distiller, Daniel Weller, became a whiskey trader in 1849 and sold his bourbon as "Honest Whiskey at an Honest Price." Around 1900, the Weller company became associated with Louisville distillers Frederick and Philip Stitzel, and by 1912, the Weller company was using the Stitzel's distillery to make their own whiskey. During Prohibition, when their whiskey was sold as medicinal stock, the two companies merged and the Stitzel-Weller company came into existence.

W. L. WELLER SPECIAL RESERVE, 7 YEARS OLD, 45% ABV

RATING: 90

A sweet honeyed nose with a nice balance of fruits and spices as the backdrop; the body is medium and the palate is buttery rich with notes of honey, berries, vanilla, and a potpourri of spices that take a backseat; the finish is long and buttery.

Overall: A great whiskey that's underappreciated by most in America. Sip it neat or on the rocks.

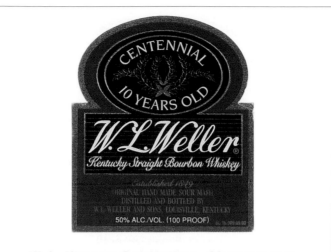

W. L. WELLER CENTENNIAL, 10 YEARS OLD, 50% ABV

RATING: 97

An intensely complex, fruity nose that switches among vanilla, dried fruits, and just a dash of mixed spices; the body is huge and the palate follows along the line of the nose with an abundance of rich vanilla, a basketful of lush fruits, and a wonderful butterscotch backdrop; the finish is long and incredibly sophisticated and understated.

Overall: One of the best whiskeys in America today. Sip it neat or on the rocks.

Woodford Reserve Distiller's Select Bourbon

DISTILLERY: The Labrot & Graham Distillery, Versailles, Kentucky

THE WHISKEY: You can learn more about this plant and its tremendous historical importance on page 160. Here we should just mention that, since this distillery didn't start production until 1996, the whiskey in the bottles of Woodford Reserve available prior to the year 2002, comes from a very specially selected batch of barrels made by Labrot & Graham's master distiller.

WOODFORD RESERVE DISTILLER'S SELECT, 45.2% ABV

RATING: 91

An intense vanilla-caramel nose also bears a rich backdrop of old leather; the body is huge and almost chewy and the palate offers toffee notes, a touch of butterscotch, and just like the nose, notes of rich leather with a hint of tobacco thrown in for good measure; the finish is very long and smooth.

Overall: A really great whiskey. Sip it neat or on the rocks.

Yellowstone Bourbon

BOTTLER AND MARKETER: The David Sherman Company, St. Louis, Missouri

THE WHISKEY: This brand name was introduced in or around 1872 when Yellowstone National Park was first opened. The originator of the whiskey was J. B. Dant, son of J. W. Dant who had been in the whiskey business since 1836. This whiskey was available by prescription during Prohibition and is said to have been Kentucky's favorite brand during the 1960s. The brand name is now owned by the David Sherman Company.

YELLOWSTONE BOURBON, 45% ABV

RATING: 86

A sweet vanilla nose with a fruity backdrop that's made more interesting by a hint of spice and clover; the medium body bears a palate rich with caramel and fruits; the finish, unfortunately, is a little on the short side but it has a nice, sharp bite.

Overall: When we first tasted this whiskey a few years ago, we deemed it to be merely mediocre, but now it seems to be a little more complex than previous bottlings. Sip it on the rocks.

PART III

A - Z Directory
of
American Distilleries

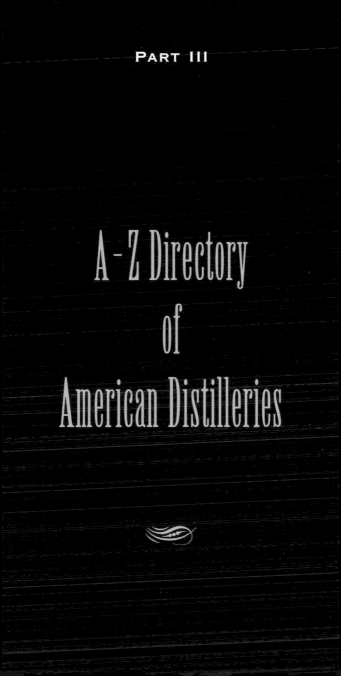

THE ANCIENT AGE DISTILLERY

AKA THE LEESTOWN DISTILLERY;
AKA THE BLANTON DISTILLERY
Leestown, Kentucky

Straight Whiskeys:
Ancient Age Bourbons
Benchmark Bourbons
Benchmark XO Single-Barrel Bourbon
Blanton's Single-Barrel Bourbon
Eagle Rare Bourbon
Elmer T. Lee Single-Barrel Bourbon
Hancock's Reserve Single-Barrel Bourbon
Rock Hill Farms Single-Barrel Bourbon

HISTORY

A distillery has existed on this site, fairly close to downtown Frankfort since 1865, when Benjamin Harrison Blanton, a retired Confederate Army officer, settled at what was then called Rock Hill Farm. After starting out as a farmer-distiller, he soon established the O. F. C. (Old Fire Copper) Distillery on his land.

Colonel Edmund Haynes Taylor Jr., one of the men responsible for the Bottled-in-Bond Act of 1897, and George T. Stagg, another notable nineteenth-century whiskey man, were both involved with this plant, but in 1897, Albert B. Blanton, Benjamin's son, went to work here, and by 1912 he had become the distillery manager.

Although the distillery didn't have a license to distill medicinal whiskey during Prohibition, the bottling house was used during the dry years. During Prohibition, Blanton was made president of the distillery, which was expanded to its present size sometime between Repeal (1933) and 1940. In 1953 the distillery was renamed The Albert B. Blanton Distillery, and it is now known variously as the Blanton Distillery, the Leestown Distillery, and the Ancient Age Distillery.

PRODUCTION

Mashbill: Corn=80%, rye=10%, barley malt=10%
Water Source: Filtered Kentucky River water, adjusted for mineral content

ELMER T. LEE, MASTER DISTILLER EMERITUS AT THE ANCIENT AGE DISTILLERY

Fermenters: Copper-bearing steel
Sour Mash: 33% of the total mash
Yeast Strain: Schenley strain of dried yeast
Secondary Still: Doubler
Proof: Whiskey leaves the doubler at around 67% abv
Entered into barrels at: 62.5% abv
Barrel Char: #3
Warehouses: Multistory warehouses, heated and cooled during colder weather. (Barrels destined to become Blanton's Single-Barrel Bourbon are aged separately in a four-story warehouse constructed of metal-clad wood. It's the only heated metal-clad warehouse in Kentucky.)
Filtration: Most whiskeys are filtered at room temperature,

but the single-barrel bottlings are chill-filtered and bottled in a special bottling room that is a regular stop on the distillery tour.

Master Distiller Emeritus: Elmer Tandy Lee
Master Distiller: Gary Gayheart

THE A. SMITH BOWMAN DISTILLERY

Fredericksburg, Virginia

Straight Whiskeys:
Virginia Gentleman Bourbons

HISTORY

A. Smith Bowman Sr., formerly the owner of a motor coach company, became a farmer in 1927 when he bought a 7,000-acre Virginia property known as Sunset Hills. Bowman switched hats again when he built a distillery on his farm after Repeal. A. Smith Bowman Sr. died in 1952, and his sons, A. Smith Bowman Jr. and E. DeLong Bowman, took over the company.

Illustrious people such as Robert E. Lee IV, great-grandson of General Robert E. Lee, and John "Jay" Buchanan Adams Jr., distantly related to three U. S. presidents—John and John Quincy Adams and Jefferson—now preside over this distillery which, in 1988, moved to Fredericksburg, on the banks of the Rappahannock River.

PRODUCTION

Mashbill: Corn=65%, rye=20%, barley malt=15%
Note: This distillery commissions low wines to be made at another location, and therefore some details included for other distilleries are omitted here.
Sour Mash: Yes, percentage unavailable
Yeast Strain: Not available
Secondary Still: Doubler
Entered into barrels at: 62.5% abv
Barrel Char: #2
Warehouses: One-story, heated, brick warehouses, stacked 3 to 4 barrels high
Filtration: Chill filtered
Master Distiller: Joseph H. Dangler

THE BARTON DISTILLERY

Bardstown, Kentucky

Straight Whiskeys:
Very Old Barton Bourbons
Kentucky Gentleman Bourbons
Ten High Bourbon
Colonel Lee Bourbon
Tom Moore Bourbons
Barclay's Bourbon
Kentucky Tavern Bourbon

HISTORY

A distillery has been located on this site since 1889 when Tom Moore, a man who started out in the whiskey business some 13 years previously, established the Tom Moore Distillery. Tom Moore himself operated his distillery right up until Prohibition forced the plant to close. When the plant reopened in 1934, the new owner, Harry Teur, renamed it the Barton Distillery, although nobody there seems to know where the name originated.

Ten years later the distillery was taken over by Oscar Getz, author of *Whiskey: An American Pictorial History* and founder of what is now known as The Oscar Getz Museum of Whiskey History. The museum, originally on the grounds of the distillery, is now in Spalding Hall, right in the center of Bardstown, and is well worth a trip.

THE SINGLE-BARREL BOTTLING HOUSE AT ANCIENT AGE DISTILLERY.

THE BOTTLING LINE AT BARTON BRANDS.

PRODUCTION

Mashbill: Corn=75%, rye= 15%, barley malt=10%

Water Source: A small percentage of the water comes from a nearby spring, the rest is from the spring-fed Teur's Lake.

Fermenters: Steel

Sour Mash: 20% of the total mash

Yeast Strain: 1940s strain not propagated on premises

Secondary Still: Doubler

Proof: Whiskey leaves the doubler at about 67.5% abv

Entered into barrels at: 62.5% abv

Barrel Char: #3

Warehouses: Multistory, unheated warehouses

Filtration: Chill filtered

Master Distiller: William Friel

THE BERNHEIM DISTILLERY

Louisville, Kentucky

Straight Whiskeys:
Old Charter Bourbons
I. W. Harper Bourbons
James E. Pepper Bourbon (export only)
W. L. Weller Bourbons (wheated)
Old Fitzgerald Bourbons (wheated)
Rebel Yell Bourbon (wheated)

HISTORY

The Bernheim Distillery, named for I. W. Bernheim, creator of I. W. Harper bourbon, opened in 1992 and the control rooms here resemble Cape Canaveral—monitors display each and every part of the distillation process in real time so the distillers can know exactly what's going on at each stage. However, as modern as this facility is, they still use a thumper for their secondary distillation—a procedure harking back to the old moonshiners of Kentucky.

In 1997 The Classic Kentucky Bourbon Company was established with the mandate to take new bourbon bottlings into the ever-expanding global markets. Several, new, extra-aged bottlings are set for release, many derived from stocks that were made at American distilleries that are now silent, or closed.

PRODUCTION

Mashbill: Corn=86%, rye=6%, barley malt=8%
Wheated Mashbill: Corn=75%, wheat=20%, barley malt=5%
Water Source: Filtered city water, adjusted for mineral content
Fermenters: Stainless steel
Sour Mash: 25% of the total mash
Yeast Strain: Schenley strain developed during or just after Prohibition
Secondary Still: Thumper
Proof: Regular whiskey leaves the thumper at about 70% abv; wheated whiskey leaves the thumper at about 65% abv
Entered into barrels at: Regular whiskey: 62.5% abv; wheated whiskey: 56% abv
Barrel Char: #3
Warehouses: Regular whiskey is stored in multistory, heated, brick warehouses; wheated whiskey is aged in multistory, iron-clad, unheated warehouses.
Filtration: Regular whiskey is chill filtered; wheated whiskey is filtered at room temperature.
Master Distiller Emeritus: Edwin S. Foote
Master Distiller: Michael Wright

THE BERNHEIM DISTILLERY, LOUISVILLE, KENTUCKY, CIRCA 1960.

THE CHARLES MEDLEY DISTILLERY

Owensboro, Kentucky

Straight Whiskey:
Wathens Kentucky Bourbon
(single-barrel, though not noted on label)

HISTORY

Charles Medley, president of this company, is a direct descendant of John Medley, an Englishman who arrived on these shores with his family and a still in 1634. In 1800, John Medley VI moved to Kentucky, and some twelve years later the Medley Distilling Company was formed. The Medleys are related through marriage to the Wathens, another great Kentucky distilling family who were responsible for keeping the Old Grand-Dad label alive.

Seven generations of Medleys owned various commercial distilleries from 1812 right up until 1959. Until 1991, a Medley always has been employed as a Master Distiller. Now the Medleys are back in business at this plant that opened in 1996.

PRODUCTION

Mashbill: Corn=77%, rye=10%, barley malt=13%
Water Source: Nearby deep wells
Fermenters: Stainless steel
Sour Mash: 27% of total mash
Yeast Strain: Medley family strain propagated on premises in dona tubs using a sour wine yeast process
Secondary Still: All-copper doubler
Proof: Whiskey leaves the doubler at around 66.5% abv
Entered into barrels at: 58.5% abv
Barrel Char: #3
Warehouses: Four-story, unheated, masonry warehouses and six-story, metal-clad warehouses
Filtration: Room temperature
Master Distiller: Charles Medley

THE EARLY TIMES DISTILLERY

Louisville, Kentucky

Straight Whiskeys:
Early Times Straight Bourbons (export only)
Old Forester Bourbons

HISTORY

The original Early Times Distillery was opened by John Beam in 1860, at a site close to Bardstown. Before the turn of the century it was producing Early Times, A. G. Nall, and Jack Beam whiskeys. The distillery closed in 1920 because of Prohibition and was bought by its present owners, Brown-Forman, during America's dry years. Brown-Forman held a license to market medicinal spirits during Prohibition, and existing stocks, distilled before 1920, were sold by prescription until Repeal in 1933.

The present distillery in Louisville opened after Prohibition and is very factory-like in appearance. However, the distillers still cultivate their own strain of yeast, and they still use an old-fashioned thumper for their secondary distillation.

PRODUCTION

Mashbill: Early Times: Corn=79%, rye=11%, barley malt=10%

Old Forester: Corn=72%, rye=18%, barley malt=10%

Water Source: Filtered city water, adjusted for mineral content

Fermenters: Carbon steel

Sour Mash: 20% of the total mash

Yeast Strain: Propagated on premises in dona tubs and soured with lactic bacteria

Secondary Still: Thumper

Proof: Whiskey leaves the thumper at about 70% abv

OLD FORESTER, THE FIRST BOURBON TO BE SOLD EXCLUSIVELY IN SEALED BOTTLES.

Entered into barrels at: 62.5% abv
Barrel Char: #3
Warehouses: Multistory warehouses, heated and cooled during colder weather
Filtration: Room temperature
Master Distiller: Lincoln Henderson

THE FOUR ROSES DISTILLERY
Lawrenceburg, Kentucky

Straight Whiskeys:
Four Roses Straight Bourbons (export only)
Four Roses Single-Barrel Reserve
Cougar Bourbon (made in Kentucky, bottled in Australia)

HISTORY

According to documents recently discovered by whiskey historian Michael Veach, Paul Jones, the creator of the Four Roses brand, started in the whiskey and tobacco business in Georgia shortly after the Civil War. At some time around 1886, Georgia enacted a statewide prohibition, and Jones moved his business to Kentucky. He died in 1895 at age 54, and in true distiller fashion was buried in a copper-lined casket.

In the mid-1940s Joseph E. Seagram and Sons Ltd. bought

THE HOME OF FOUR ROSES BOURBON.

the Four Roses brand name and the Four Roses Distillery, a plant that had been known at various times as the Old Joe Distillery and the Old Prentice Distillery. This plant is of Spanish design, and passersby could be excused if they thought they had stumbled upon an old mission similar to those found in California or the Southwest.

PRODUCTION

Mashbill: Proprietary
Water Source: Spring water
Fermenters: Mostly cypress, some stainless steel
Sour Mash: 25% of the total mash
Yeast Strain: Several different yeast strains used, propagated in dona tubs and soured with lactic bacteria
Secondary Still: Doubler
Proof: Whiskey leaves the doubler at 71.5% abv
Entered into barrels at: 60% abv
Barrel Char: #3.5
Warehouses: Single-story, unheated, metal-clad warehouses
Filtration: Chill filtered
Master Distiller Emeritus: Ova Haney
Master Distiller: Jim Rutledge

GEORGE A. DICKEL'S CASCADE DISTILLERY

Tullahoma, Tennessee

Straight Whiskey:
George A. Dickel's Tennessee Sour-Mash Whiskies
George A. Dickel's Special Barrel Reserve Tennessee Whisky
George A. Dickel's Vintage-Dated Tennessee Whisky
(export only)
George A. Dickel's Rx Cascade Bourbon (export only)

HISTORY

The Cascade Distillery was founded by two men named Brown and Cunningham in 1877, and it quickly became a favorite with George A. Dickel, a German immigrant whisky retailer in Tennessee since 1866. By 1881 Dickel had formed a company with his brother-in-law, Victor Schwab, and some seven years later the company had gained controlling interest in the Cascade Distillery which, at the time, was producing Cascade Whisky, promoted as being "Mellow as Moonlight."

George Dickel died in 1894, but his company kept control of the distillery, and by 1904, the Cascade Distillery had become the largest distillery in the state. In 1910, a decade before national Prohibition, Tennessee declared statewide prohibition, and production of Cascade whisky was moved to Louisville, Kentucky. Yet even though this whisky was being produced in Kentucky, it was still made using the Lincoln County Process—slowly filtered through huge vats of sugar-maple charcoal. Thus, the whisky retained its distinctive Tennessee style and flavor.

Although Cascade whisky survived national Prohibition and was back on the market by 1935, the Tullahoma distillery lay in a state of disrepair until just after World War II. Ralph Dupps, a master distiller, was hired to rebuild the distillery on the original site and did so, using the original plans. The whisky, however, didn't bear George Dickel's name until 1964; prior to then, it was known only as Cascade whisky.

PRODUCTION
Mashbill: Corn=80%, rye=12%, barley malt=8%
Water Source: Spring water
Fermenters: Stainless steel
Sour Mash: 25% of the total mash
Yeast Strain: Dried yeast
Secondary Still: Doubler
Proof: Whisky leaves the doubler at about 65% abv
Lincoln County Process: The new spirit is chilled and entered into 10-foot-deep vats of sugar-maple charcoal until they are completely full. Then the whisky is slowly drained from the bottom of the tank while more new spirit is dripped in from the top.
Entered into barrels at: 57.5% abv
Barrel Char: #3
Warehouses: One-story warehouses, heated only when necessary to maintain a low temperature of 55°F
Filtration: Chill filtered
Master Distiller: David Backus

The Heaven Hill Distillery

Bardstown, Kentucky

Straight Whiskeys:
Heaven Hill Bourbons
Evan Williams Bourbons
Elijah Craig Bourbons
Henry McKenna Bourbons
J. T. S. Brown Bourbon
J. W. Dant Bourbon
Mattingly & Moore Bourbon
T. W. Samuels Bourbon
Daniel Stewart Bourbon
Cabin Still Bourbon
Echo Springs Bourbon

History

This distillery opened in 1935 when a group of business-men decided to take advantage of the end of Prohibition. Five members of the Shapira family were among the investors, and they were left holding the distillery when some of the core group dropped out of the business. Unfortunately, according to the present-day president of the company, Max Shapira, his forefathers "didn't know a barrel from a box." They learned, though, quite quickly, the ins and outs of the whiskey business.

OLD HEAVEN HILL SPRINGS DISTILLERY, BARDSTOWN, KENTUCKY.

This distillery, named for William Heavenhill, a farmer who previously owned the land on which the plant is built, is a family-owned distillery, and to their credit, the Shapira's employ members of the Beam family to make their whiskeys. The father-and-son team of Parker and Craig Beam still cultivate their own yeast at the distillery.

PRODUCTION
Mashbill: Corn=75%, rye=13%, barley malt=12%
Water Source: Spring-fed lakes
Fermenters: 4 cypress; 27 stainless steel
Sour Mash: 25% of the total mash
Yeast Strain: Propagated on premises in dona tubs with hops used in the yeast mash
Secondary Still: Doubler
Proof: Whiskey leaves the doubler at around 69% abv
Entered into barrels at: 62.5% abv
Barrel Char: #3
Warehouses: Multistory, unheated, metal-clad warehouses
Filtration: Chill filtered
Master Distiller: Parker Beam
Assistant Distiller: Craig Beam

THE JACK DANIEL DISTILLERY
Lynchburg, Tennessee

Straight Whiskeys:
Jack Daniel's No. 7 Brand Tennessee
Sour Mash Whiskey
Jack Daniel's Old No. 7 Brand Tennessee
Sour Mash Whiskey
Gentleman Jack Rare Tennessee Whiskey
Jack Daniel's Single-Barrel Tennessee Whiskey

HISTORY
This distillery claims to be the "oldest registered distillery in the U.S.A.," and it was on this site that Jack Daniel, reputedly a distiller since he was fourteen years old, set up his own plant in 1866. The land was known as The Hollow at Cave Spring and is said to be the site at which Alfred Eaton created the Tennessee whiskey mellowing process known as the

BARRELS OF JACK DANIEL'S ON THE WAY TO WAREHOUSES FOR AGING.

Lincoln County Process (the practice of filtering whiskey through vats of sugar-maple charcoal before it is entered into barrels for aging).

In the early 1880s Jack's nephew, Lem Motlow, was employed at the distillery and soon became manager of the plant. In 1907 Jack turned the company over to his cousin, Dick Daniel, and Lem Motlow, who soon bought Daniel's shares and took over completely.

In 1910, when Tennessee declared statewide prohibition, Motlow opened a distillery in St. Louis, and two years later he opened another distillery in Birmingham, Alabama. Although Prohibition ended in 1933, it wasn't until 1938 that Motlow got permission from the state of Tennessee to fire up the stills at the original distillery in Lynchburg.

Lem Motlow died in 1947, and his sons, Reagor, Robert, Daniel, and Clifford (known as the "Shirtsleeve Brothers"), took control of the company. Brown-Forman, owners of Early Times and Old Forester Kentucky whiskeys, bought the Jack Daniel's Distillery in the 1950s and continue to operate it today.

PRODUCTION
Mashbill: Corn=80%, rye=12%, barley malt=8%
Water Source: Spring water
Fermenters: Stainless steel
Sour Mash: 20% of the total mash
Yeast Strain: Dried yeast
Secondary Still: Thumper
Proof: Whiskey leaves the thumper at about 70% abv
Lincoln County Process: New spirit is chilled and dripped over about 10 feet of sugar-maple charcoal. (Whiskey destined to be bottled as Gentleman Jack Rare Tennessee Whiskey undergoes this process twice—once before barreling, and once after aging.)
Entered into barrels at: 59% abv
Barrel Char: #3
Warehouses: Multistory, unheated warehouses
Filtration: Chill filtered
Master Distiller: Jimmy Bedford

THE JIM BEAM DISTILLERY

Clermont and Boston, Kentucky

Straight Whiskeys:
Jim Beam Bourbons
Old Taylor Bourbon
Old Crow Bourbon
Old Grand-Dad Bourbons
Booker's Small-Batch Bourbon
Knob Creek Small-Batch Bourbon
Baker's Small-Batch Bourbon
Basil Hayden Small-Batch Bourbon
Jacob's Well Twice-Barreled Bourbon

HISTORY

Jim Beam is probably the best-known bourbon name in the world, and the Beams (originally Boehm) have been making whiskey in Kentucky since at least 1895. Jacob Boehm was a German immigrant who made his way to Kentucky around 1785 and set up his still shortly thereafter, eventually establishing a commercial distillery and teaching his sons, David and John, the ways of the still.

David Beam eventually took over his father's plant, then known as the Old Tub Distillery, while John went on to open the Early Times Distillery in 1860. Jim Beam, born James Beauregard Beam, took over the distillery in 1892 and continued to run the plant with his brother-in-law/partner, Albert J. Hart, until 1919 when the shadow of Prohibition forced them to close the doors.

The James B. Beam Distilling Company was formed in 1933, and once again Jim Beam, along with his son, Jeremiah Beam, began making their bourbon, and although the company has changed hands a couple of times since then—it's now owned by the Jim Beam Brands Company—there has always been a Beam at the helm of the stills. Jim Beam's nephew, Carl, and Carl's son, Baker, both worked at this plant, and Booker Noe (Jim's grandson) is not only the present day Master Distiller Emeritus, he's also one of the most colorful and delightful men in the business.

Booker admits to howling at the moon when he's with friends, and has taught us much about the art of distillation.

PRODUCTION

Mashbill: Proprietary

Water Source: Spring-fed lake

Fermenters: Stainless steel

Sour Mash: 41% of the total mash

Yeast Strain: Propagated on premises in dona tubs with hops used in the yeast mash

Secondary Still: Doubler

Proof: Whiskey leaves the doubler at around 62.5% abv

Entered into barrels at: 62.5% abv

Barrel Char: #4

Warehouses: Multistory, unheated, all-wood and metal-clad wooden warehouses

Filtration: Chill-filtered, however, Booker's Bourbon is a completely unfiltered product

Master Distiller Emeritus: Booker Noe

THE LABROT & GRAHAM DISTILLERY

Versailles, Kentucky

Straight Whiskeys:
Woodford Reserve Distiller's Select Bourbon
President's Choice Bourbon (export only)

HISTORY

Although whiskey has been produced on this site since as early as 1812, this distillery is the very place where noted nineteenth-century distiller James Crow perfected the sour-mash method of making whiskey sometime between 1823 and 1845. When Crow was in residence, the plant was known as the Old Oscar Pepper Distillery, and the whiskeys made there were acclaimed by such major figures as Ulysses S. Grant and Henry Clay.

The distillery went through a few changes in ownership, including a period when it was owned by Edmund H. Taylor, the man mainly responsible for the passage of the Bottled-in-Bond Act of 1897. The plant was purchased in 1878 by James Graham and Leopold Labrot, hence the name of the present distillery. Labrot & Graham is owned by Brown-Forman, the Louisville company that produces Old Forester and Early Times whiskeys, who rebuilt and restored the distillery to its current splendor, smack dab in the center of the breathtakingly beautiful bluegrass horse country. Whiskey production started in 1996, and at the time of writing, the bourbon that is aging in the air-dried wood barrels stacked in the property's warehouses is the only bourbon made entirely in pot stills.

PRODUCTION

Note: Bottlings of Woodford Reserve bourbon available at the time of writing are filled with whiskey made at Brown-Forman's Early Times Distillery in Louisville. However, this whiskey is neither Early Times, nor the company's other bottling, Old Forester; it is a mingling of special barrels of whiskey that have matured particularly well and fit the flavor profile that has become known as the signature style for Woodford Reserve. The following information pertains to the whiskey that is currently being produced at this plant which won't be available to the public until at least 2002.

Mashbill: Experimental at present
Water Source: Nearby natural well
Fermenters: Cypress
Sour Mash: Quantities used are experimental at present
Yeast Strain: Propagated on premises in dona tubs and soured with their own strain of lactic bacteria
Stills: Triple distilled in specially designed copper pot stills
Proof: Whiskey leaves the third still at about 79% abv
Entered into barrels at: 55% abv
Barrel Char: #3
Warehouses: Four- to five-story, heated
Filtration: Room temperature
Master Distiller: Lincoln Henderson

MAKER'S MARK DISTILLERY

Loretto, Kentucky

Straight Whisky:
Maker's Mark Bourbon (wheated)
Maker's Mark Limited Edition (wheated, for export only)
Maker's Mark Select Bourbon (wheated, for export only)

HISTORY

Bill Samuels Jr., president of Maker's Mark, is descended

from Robert Samuels, a whiskey distiller in Kentucky in 1780 (and prior to that date, a distiller in Pennsylvania). The Samuels family has been making bourbon ever since: Robert Samuel's son, William, distilled whiskey, and his son, Taylor William Samuels, established the family's first commercial distillery in 1844. The Samuels family has a long tradition of prominence in Kentucky—Taylor served four terms as a High Sheriff, and his son, William Isaac Samuels, was president of the Nelson County Agricultural and Fair Organization, the Bardstown and Shepherdsville Turnpike Company, and the Kentucky Swine Breeders Association.

William's son, Leslie Samuels, ran the distillery until Prohibition in 1920, and after Repeal in 1933, he built a new plant in Deatsville, and reopened the T. W. Samuels Distillery. This plant was eventually taken over by Leslie's son, T. William Samuels, who ran it until 1943 when, for the first time since 1780, the family dropped out of the whiskey business and sold the distillery.

Ten years later, T. William Samuels bought a small distillery in Loretto (a plant established in 1805), and restored every square inch of the place with great attention to historical detail. The distillery is now a National Historic Landmark.

Maker's Mark distillery boasts a "Quart House"—a small store where their whisky was sold at retail—a toll house, and two of its bonded warehouses date to the last century. The plant is situated in Marion County, Kentucky, and is probably the most picturesque distillery in the state.

PRODUCTION

Mashbill: Corn=70%, wheat=16%, barley malt=14%

Water Source: Spring water

Fermenters: Cypress and stainless steel

Sour Mash: 32% of the total mash

Yeast Strain: Propagated on premises in dona tubs with hops used in the yeast mash

Secondary Still: Doubler

Proof: Whisky leaves the doubler at about 65% abv

Entered into barrels at: 55% abv

Barrel Char: #3

Warehouses: Multistory, unheated warehouses; barrels are rotated regularly

Filtration: Room temperature

Master Distiller: Steve Nally

THE WILD TURKEY DISTILLERY

Lawrenceburg, Kentucky

Straight Whiskeys:
Wild Turkey Bourbons
Wild Turkey Kentucky Spirit Single-Barrel Bourbon
Wild Turkey Rare Breed Small-Batch Bourbon

HISTORY

This distillery was once known as the Old Moore Distillery, and was bought, in 1905, by the four Ripy brothers, sons of Thomas B. Ripy, a distiller in Kentucky since at least 1869. The distillery was closed during Prohibition but in 1934, after Repeal, the Ripy brothers reopened the plant, and although they sold it soon afterward, the Ripys continued to work at the distillery. This plant was bought, in 1970, by Austin, Nichols & Company, Inc., a company that started producing its own line of distilled spirits soon after Repeal.

Jimmy Russell, the Master Distiller at Wild Turkey, worked with and was trained by a member of the Ripy family. He is the embodiment of a true whiskey man.

PRODUCTION

Mashbill: Corn=75%, rye=13%, barley malt=12%
Water Source: Spring-fed lake

A MIDSUMMER DAY AT MAKER'S MARK DISTILLERY.

THE WILD TURKEY DISTILLERY.

Fermenters: Cypress and stainless steel

Sour Mash: 33% of the total mash

Yeast Strain: Propagated on premises in dona tubs and soured with lactic bacteria

Secondary Still: Doubler

Proof: Whiskey leaves the doubler at between 60 and 62.5% abv

Entered into barrels at: Between 52.5 and 53.5% abv

Barrel Char: #4

Warehouses: Multistory, unheated, metal-clad warehouses; barrels are rotated periodically

Filtration: Room temperature; the 80-proof bottling is chill filtered

Master Distiller: Jimmy Russell

Visiting the Distilleries

Travelers can visit eight of the thirteen distilleries located in Kentucky and Tennessee. (The A. Smith Bowman Distillery in Virginia does not offer tours at this time.) Many of the visitor centers at the plants feature videotaped presentations, historical displays, graphic representations of the whiskey-making process, and well-stocked gift shops. Guided tours of the distilleries usually vary from thirty to sixty minutes in length; some are a start-to-finish look at the process from the grain-receiving docks and dona rooms to warehouses and bottling lines, while others hit the high points, take in the scenery, and leave ample time for questions.

Once you've seen one distillery, don't think you've seen them all; each is different in its own way. Several properties have historical structures on site that have been beautifully restored. A few even have meeting facilities suitable for presentations or corporate meetings, and the distilleries try to make special provisions for larger groups.

None of the distilleries charge for their tours. All are closed on major holidays.

Kentucky:

Jim Beam's Visitor Center and Distillery
Clermont, Kentucky 40110
502-543-9877

Heaven Hill Distillery
Highway 49, Loretto Road (P.O. Box 729)
Bardstown, Kentucky 40004-0729
502-348-3921
Tours on weekdays only.

Maker's Mark Distillery
Loretto, Kentucky 40037
502-865-2099
*Six tours a day Mondays through Saturdays and
three afternoon tours on Sundays.*

THE OSCAR GETZ MUSEUM OF WHISKEY HISTORY IN SPALDING HALL,
BARDSTOWN, KENTUCKY.

The Oscar Getz Museum of Whiskey History and The Bardstown Historical Museum
Spalding Hall
114 North Fifth Street
Bardstown, KY 40004
502-348-2999
*A delightful museum that has much to teach
those who are interested in the history of bourbon
and American whiskeys.*

The Ancient Age Distillery/The Leestown Company
1001 Wilkinson Boulevard
Frankfort, Kentucky 40601
502-223-7641
*Tours are offered from Monday through Friday
between 9:00 A.M. and 2:00 P.M.*

The Wild Turkey Distillery
Highway 1510, Box 180
Lawrenceburg, Kentucky 40342
502-839-4544
*Tours are available four times a day, Mondays through
Fridays. Closed to visitors during the last two weeks
of July and the first week of January.*

The Labrot & Graham Distillery
7855 McCracken Pike
Versailles, Kentucky 40383
606-879-1812
*Your chance to see the only copper pot stills in Kentucky.
Five tours every day: Tuesdays through Saturdays
from April through October; Wednesdays through Saturdays
from November through March.*

TENNESSEE:

George A. Dickel's Cascade Distillery
Cascade Hollow (P. O. Box 490)
Tullahoma, Tennessee 37388
615-857-3124
*Free tours are conducted Mondays through Fridays
from 9:00 A.M. to 3:00 P.M.*

Jack Daniel's Distillery
Highway 55 (P.O. Box 199)
Lynchburg, Tennessee 37352
615-759-4221
*Frequent tours are available daily.
Be sure to reserve for lunch at Miss Mary Bobo's Boarding
House (three doors west of the Moore County Jail),
Lynchburg, TN 37352; 615-759-7394.*

WHISKEY SOCIETIES AND NEWSLETTERS

These are a few clubs and newsletters organized and written strictly for bourbon and whiskey enthusiasts.

The Bardstown Bourbon Society
P.O. Box 817
Bardstown, KY 40004-9971
Write for membership materials.

The Kentucky Bourbon Circle
P. O. Box 1
Clermont, KY 40110-9980
For free membership, call 800-6KBCIRCLE
(1-800-652-2472) or write for details.

Single-Barrel Bourbon Society
P. O. Box 1031
Louisville, KY 40201
Free membership, write for details.

Wild Turkey Rare Breed Society
c/o Jimmy Russell, Master Distiller
Wild Turkey Distillery
1525 Tyrone Road
Lawrenceburg, KY 40342

The Bourbon Country Reader
3712 North Broadway
Box 298
Chicago, IL 60613
Send a stamped, self-addressed envelope for a free
issue and subscription details.

F. Paul Pacult's Spirit Journal
241 Old Reservoir Rd.
Wallkill, NY 12589
Subscriptions available.

A QUICK GUIDE TO WHISKEY RATINGS

EXCELLENT (96+)

Booker's Bourbon

Four Roses Single-Barrel Reserve

Old Charter Proprietor's Reserve, 13 years old

Old Rip Van Winkle, 15 years old

Pappy Van Winkle Family Reserve Kentucky Straight
Bourbon, 20 years old

*Stitzel-Weller Rare Bourbon, 17 years old

Very Special Old Fitzgerald, 12 years old

Wild Turkey Kentucky Spirit

Wild Turkey Rare Breed

W. L. Weller Centennial, 10 years old

HIGHLY RECOMMENDED (91–95)

A. H. Hirsch Reserve Pot-Stilled Sour Mash Straight
Bourbon, 16 years old

A. H. Hirsch Pot-Stilled Sour Mash Straight Bourbon,
20 years old

Eagle Rare Bourbon, 10 years old

Elijah Craig Single-Barrel Bourbon, 18 years old

Elmer T. Lee Single-Barrel Bourbon

Evan Williams Single-Barrel Bourbon, Vintage 1989

*Four Roses Super Premium Bourbon

I. W. Harper, 12 years old

I. W. Harper Gold Medal, 15 years old

Jim Beam Black, 7 years old

Joseph Finch Rare Bourbon, 15 years old

Maker's Mark

*Maker's Mark Limited Edition

*Maker's Mark Select

Old Charter, The Classic 90, 12 years old

Old Forester Bonded

*Denotes bottlings that are for export only.

Old Grand-Dad 114 Barrel Proof
Old Rip Van Winkle Bourbon, 10 summers old
*Taylor & Williams Rare Bourbon, 17 years old
Wathen's Kentucky Bourbon
Wild Turkey Old Number 8 Brand
Wild Turkey, 12 years old
Woodford Reserve Distiller's Select

RECOMMENDED (86–90)

Ancient Ancient Age, 10 years old
Baker's Bourbon, 7 years old
Basil Hayden's Bourbon, 8 years old
Beam's Choice
*Benchmark XO Single-Barrel Bourbon
Blanton's Single-Barrel Bourbon
*Early Times Straight Bourbon
Elijah Craig, 12 years old
Evan Williams, 7 years old
Evan Williams Single-Barrel Bourbon, Vintage 1988
*Four Roses Bourbon
*Four Roses Fine Old Bourbon
Gentleman Jack Rare Tennessee Whiskey
George Dickel Old No. 8 Brand
George Dickel No. 12 Superior Brand
George Dickel Special Barrel Reserve, 10 years old
Hancock's Reserve Single-Barrel Bourbon
Henry Clay Rare Bourbon, 16 years old
Henry McKenna 10-year-old Single-Barrel Bourbon
I. W. Harper
*I. W. Harper President's Reserve
Knob Creek, 9 years old
Old Charter, 8 years old
Old Charter, 10 years old
Old Ezra Rare Old Sippin' Whiskey, 7 years old
Old Fitzgerald Prime Bourbon
Old Fitzgerald Bottled-in-bond

Old Fitzgerald 1849, 8 years old
Old Forester
Old Grand-Dad
Old Grand-Dad Bottled-in-bond
Old Heaven Hill, 10 years old
Old Taylor, 6 years old
Old Weller Antique, 7 summers old
*Premium Early Times Straight Bourbon
*President's Choice
Rebel Yell
Van Winkle Special Reserve Kentucky Straight Bourbon,
12 years old
Wild Turkey
W. L. Weller Special Reserve, 7 years old
Yellowstone Kentucky Straight Bourbon

GOOD (81–85)
American Biker
Benchmark Premium Bourbon
Colonel Lee, Bottled-in-bond
Evan Williams
Ezra Brooks Kentucky Straight Bourbon
Heaven Hill, 6 years old
Jacob's Well, 84 months old
Jim Beam
Kentucky Tavern
Mattingly & Moore
Old Crow, 4 years old
Rock Hill Farms Single-Barrel Bourbon
Ten High
Very Old Barton, 6 years old
Virginia Gentleman Bourbon

FAIR (76–80)
Jack Daniel's Old No. 7 Brand (Black label)
Jack Daniel's Single-Barrel Tennessee Whiskey

Tom Moore, Bottled-in-bond
Very Old Barton Bottled-in-bond, 4 years old

POOR (75 AND BELOW)
Ancient Age
Barclay's
Cabin Still Bourbon
Daniel Stewart
Echo Springs Bourbon
Heaven Hill
Henry McKenna
Jack Daniel's No. 7 Brand (green label)
*James E. Pepper
J. T. S. Brown
J. W. Dant
Kentucky Gentleman, 6 years old
Tom Moore
T. W. Samuels Bourbon
Walker's DeLuxe Straight Bourbon

GLOSSARY

ABV: The abreviation for alcohol by volume. The amount is expressed as a percentage of 100.

BACKSET: Liquid strained from the mash after its primary distillation. Sometimes referred to as sour mash, stillage, spent beer, or setback.

BARRELS: In American whiskey terms, closed, liquid-tight, wooden casks constructed from oak. Their interiors are charred over open flames. After filling, the barrels are plugged and set on their sides for aging.

BEADING: The bubbles that form on top of whiskey in a bottle after the bottle has been shaken. Large bubbles denote high proof.

BEER: Usually called Distiller's Beer—fermented mash ready to be distilled.

BEER STILL: A continuous still used to distill low wines from distiller's beer.

BLENDED WHISKEY: Straight whiskey blended with neutral grain spirits, often with the addition of coloring and flavor enhancers.

BOTTLED-IN-BOND: A term signifying 50% abv (100°-proof) whiskey that's at least four years old.

BOURBON (STRAIGHT): A type of whiskey made from a mash containing at least 51 percent corn, distilled out at a maximum of 160 proof, aged at no more than 125 proof, for a minimum of two years in new charred oak barrels, and bottled at a minimum of 80 proof. If the whiskey is aged for less than four years, its age must be stated on the bottle. No coloring or flavoring may be added to any straight whiskey.

CHARCOAL MELLOWING: Filtration, before aging, of Tennessee whiskey through a minimum of ten feet of sugar-maple charcoal. Also known as mellowing, leaching, or the Lincoln County Process.

CHARRING: The process that sets fire to the interior of a barrel for less than one minute and creates a blackened layer of charred wood. When the barrel is filled with whiskey, the charred wood contributes color and flavors to the whiskey. Distillers can specify the degree of char they require, from #1 (the lightest) to #4 (the heaviest).

CHILL HAZE: A term used to describe the cloudiness that

appears in cold whiskey when the whiskey has undergone light filtration or no filtration at all. There is nothing wrong with a whiskey that bears a chill haze.

CONGENERS: Impurities, such as esters and fusel oils, present in minuscule amounts in beverage alcohol, that develop into rich flavors in the final, aged product.

CONTINUOUS STILL: Also known as a Coffey Still, but referred to as the beer still by American whiskey distillers who use it to distill low wines from distiller's beer.

COOPERAGE: The art of barrelmaking.

CORN WHISKEY: A whiskey made from a mash containing a minimum of 80 percent corn and, if it is aged at all, it must be aged in used or uncharred oak barrels.

DISTILLATION: Purifying the liquid part of a mixture by a series of evaporation and condensation processes.

DISTILLER'S BEER: The porridge-like, fermented mash that is transferred from the fermenter to the beer still for the first distillation.

DONA TUB: A vessel in which jug yeast is grown to produce enough yeast to ferment a whole batch of mash. (Pronounced DOE-nee or DOE-nah.)

DOUBLER: A large copper still, looking somewhat like a small water tank with an upturned funnel on top, used to distill high wines or new spirit from low wines.

DOUBLINGS: The spirit produced by a secondary distillation. Often referred to as high wines.

FERMENTER: A large vessel, made of metal (usually steel) or cypress, that contains the mash. Here, yeast (and backset) is added and the mixture ferments to create distiller's beer.

FUSEL OILS: A subcategory of congeners. Fusel oils, alcohols with a higher molecular weight than beverage alcohol, are present in minuscule amounts in beverage alcohol and add flavor to the product during aging. The presence of excess fusel oils, however, leads to a banana flavor in whiskey.

HEADS: The first quantity of the high wines to exit the doubler or thumper; this spirit is high in impurities and sent back to the still for redistillation.

HIGH WINES: The final spirit produced by the secondary distillation. At this point it is ready for aging. Sometimes called doublings.

HOPPED YEAST MASH: A mash flavored by cooked hops in which yeast is propagated.

HOPS: A member of the mulberry family, hops, in pellet form, are sometimes used to flavor the yeast mash in a dona tub.

LEACHING: Filtration, before aging, of Tennessee whiskey through a minimum of ten feet of sugar-maple charcoal. Also known as mellowing, charcoal mellowing, or the Lincoln County Process.

LINCOLN COUNTY PROCESS: The filtration of Tennessee whiskey, before it is aged, through a minimum of ten feet of sugar-maple charcoal. Sometimes referred to as mellowing, charcoal mellowing, or leaching.

LOW WINES: Spirits produced by a primary distillation, sometimes referred to as singlings.

MALT: Malted barley.

MALTED BARLEY: Barley that has been partially germinated and then heated or roasted to stop the germination. Malted barley (or any malted grain) contains enzymes not present in unmalted grains that convert starches into the fermentable sugars on which yeast feeds.

MASH: The cooked grains from the mash tub.

MASHBILL: The grain recipe used to make whiskey.

MASH TUB: A large metal vessel in which the grains are cooked prior to being transferred to the fermenter.

MELLOWING: Filtration, before aging, of Tennessee whiskey through a minimum of ten feet of sugar-maple charcoal. Also known as charcoal mellowing, leaching, or the Lincoln County Process.

MINGLING: The process in which straight whiskeys from a number of barrels are mixed together in order to achieve a consistent style of straight whiskey.

PROOF: Measurement of beverage alcohol on a scale, in America, of 200. A 100°-proof spirit contains 50 percent alcohol.

RACKHOUSE: The building in which whiskey is aged, sometimes referred to as the warehouse.

RED LAYER: A layer of caramelized tannins and wood sugars that forms within barrels during the charring process.

RICKS: The wooden structures on which barrels of whiskey rest during aging. Also—tall stacks of sugar-maple planks that are burned to produce the charcoal through which Tennessee whiskey is filtered.

RYE WHISKEY (STRAIGHT): A whiskey made from a mash containing at least 51 percent rye, distilled out at a maximum of 160 proof, and aged at no more than 125° proof for a minimum of two years in new charred oak barrels. If the whiskey is aged for less than four years, its age must be stated on the bottle. No coloring or flavoring may be added to any straight whiskey.

SINGLE-BARREL WHISKEY: Whiskey drawn from one barrel that has not been mingled with any other whiskeys.

SINGLINGS: An old moonshiner's term for low wines.

SMALL-BATCH WHISKEY: A product of mingling select barrels of whiskey that have matured into a specific style.

SMALL GRAINS: The grains other than corn, used in the production of American whiskey.

SOUR MASH: A term used to describe backset.

SOUR-MASH WHISKEY: Whiskey made from a mash to which backset has been added in the fermenter.

SOUR-YEAST MASH: A mash, usually of corn and rye, to which lactic bacteria are added before yeast is cultivated therein.

SPENT BEER: The residue of mash taken from the beer still after the first distillation.

STRAIGHT WHISKEY: A whiskey made from a mash containing at least 51 percent of any grain, distilled out at a maximum of 160 proof, and aged at no more than 125 proof for a minimum of two years in new charred oak barrels. If the whiskey is aged for less than four years, its age must be stated on the bottle. No coloring or flavoring may be added to any straight whiskey.

SWEET MASH: A mash of grains that is fermented using fresh yeast only, without the addition or help of any backset.

TAILS: The last section of high wines to exit the doubler or thumper; this spirit is high in impurities and sent back to the still for redistillation.

TENNESSEE WHISKEY (STRAIGHT): Whiskey made from a mash of at least 51 percent corn, distilled out at a maximum of 160 proof, filtered through a minimum of ten feet of sugar-maple charcoal, and then aged at no more than 125 proof for a minimum of two years in new charred oak barrels. These are not legal requirements for Tennessee whiskey, but it describes the way in which present-day Tennessee whiskeys are made. No coloring or flavoring may be added to any straight whiskey.

THUMPER: A doubler containing water through which low wine vapors are bubbled to produce high wines.

TOASTING: The process of heating the staves of a barrel over a gentle flame in order to form the shape of the barrel and convert starches in the wood into sugars that will form the red layer during the charring process.

VINTAGE WHISKEY: Whiskey that has matured particularly well and is the product of one particular season of distillation.

WAREHOUSE: The building in which whiskey is aged, sometimes referred to as the rackhouse.

WELL WHISKEY OR WELL BOURBON: A term used to describe the bottling of whiskey that is poured by a bartender when no brand name is specified.

WHEATED BOURBON: A term that we use to describe bourbon that is made from a mashbill that contains wheat instead of rye grain.

WHISKEY: A spirituous liquor distilled from a fermented mash of cooked grains.

YEAST: A living organism that feeds on fermentable sugars transforming them to beverage alcohol, congeners, carbon dioxide, and heat.

YEAST MASH: When jug yeast is grown in dona tubs, cooked grains, known as a yeast mash, are usually used as the growing medium. A yeast mash may be sweet or sour. The introduction of hops into this process produces a product that we refer to as a hopped yeast mash, and is not usually soured.

BIBLIOGRAPHY

Abraham Lincoln: His Speeches and Writings. Edited with critical and analytical notes by Roy P. Basler, New York: Da Capo Press, 1946.

Ade, George. *The Old-Time Saloon.* New York: Old Town Books, 1993.

The Anti-Saloon League Year Book, 1910. Compiled and edited by Ernest Hurst Cherrington. Ohio: The Anti-Saloon League of America Publishers, 1910.

Baker, Charles H. *The Gentleman's Companion.* New York: Crown Publishers, 1946.

Brown, John Hull. *Early American Beverages.* New York: Bonanza Books, 1966.

Crockett, Albert Stevens. *The Old Waldorf-Astoria Bar Book.* New York: A. S. Crockett, 1935.

Crowgey, Henry G. *Kentucky Bourbon The Early Years of Whiskeymaking.* Kentucky: The University Press of Kentucky, 1971.

Dabney, Joseph Earl. *Mountain Spirits, A Chronicle of Corn Whiskey from King James's Ulster Plantation to America's Appalachians and the Moonshine Life.* New York: Charles Scribner's Sons, 1974.

Downard, William L. *Dictionary of the History of the American Brewing and Distilling Industries.* Connecticut: Greenwood Press, 1980.

Earle, Alice Morse. *Home Life in Colonial Days.* (Written in 1898.) Massachusetts: The Berkshire Traveller Press, 1974.

Embury, David A. *The Fine Art of Mixing Drinks.* 2nd edition. New York: Garden City Books, 1952.

Getz, Oscar, with the collaboration of Irv. Blow. *Whiskey— An American Pictorial History.* New York: David McKay Company, Inc., 1978.

Green, Ben A. *Jack Daniel's Legacy.* Tennessee: Rich Printing Co., 1967.

Grimes, William. *Straight Up or On the Rocks—A Cultural History of American Drink.* New York: Simon & Schuster, 1993.

Harwell, Richard Barksdale. *The Mint Julep.* Virginia: University Press of Virginia, 1975.

Hibbs, Dixie. *Nelson County Kentucky: A Pictorial History.* Virginia: The Donning Company, 1989.

The Kentucky Encyclopedia. Editor in Chief, John E. Kleber. Kentucky: The University Press of Kentucky, 1992.

Kroll, Harry Harris. *Bluegrass, Belles, and Bourbon—A Pictorial History of Whiskey in Kentucky.* New Jersey: A. S. Barnes, 1967.

The Lincoln Reader. Edited, with an introduction by Paul M. Angle. New Brunswick: Rutgers University Press, 1947

A Memorial History of Louisville. Volume 1. Edited by J. Stoddard Johnston. American Biographical Publishing Company, 1896.

Pearce, John Ed. *Nothing Better In The Market.* Kentucky: Brown-Forman Distillers Corp., 1970.

Rice, Arnold S., John A. Krout & C. M. Harris. *United States History to 1877.* 8th edition. New York: HarperCollins, 1991.

Rice, Patricia M. *Altered States, Alcohol and Other Drugs in America.* Rochester, New York: The Strong Museum, 1992.

Thomas, Professor Jerry. *The Bon Vivant's Companion or How to Mix Drinks.* Edited, with an introduction by Herbert Asbury. New York: Grosset & Dunlap, 1934.

Wilson, James Boone. *The Spirit of Old Kentucky.* Kentucky: Glenmore Distilleries Company, 1945.

ACKNOWLEDGMENTS

We've been visiting Kentucky and Tennessee for a good few years, and on each successive visit it feels a little more like home. Not all the people mentioned here are in the bourbon industry, but most are, and those whiskey men and women have been invaluable during our research. If we have missed out any names, please accept our sincere apologies, and if there are any mistakes in this book, the reader should note that they are ours, and not attributable to any of the wonderful people listed here:

John "Jay" Buchanan Adams Jr., Peter Angus, Annie Armstrong, David Bachus, Craig Beam, Parker Beam, Jimmy Bedford, Joe Borders, Patty Boston, John Boswell, Roger Brashears, Mac Brown, Tom Bulleit, Jack Cavanaugh, Larry Casey, Renee Cooper, Charles Cowdery, Bill Creason, Joseph H. Dangler, Joe Darmand, Nancy DeKalb, Ralph Dupps, Barry Estabrook, Ed Foote, Louis Forman, Gary Gayheart, Melony Geary, Eve Gilbert, John Gunn, Ova Haney, Crystal Harvey, Lincoln Henderson, Dixie Hibbs, Ann T. Higgins, Mary Hite, John Holmburg, Gordon Hue, Timothy Hue, Stephen J. Hughes, Steve Kaufman, Elmer Tandy Lee, Phil Lynch, Isabel MacDonald, Rux Martin, Chris McCrory, Fred McMillen, Charles Medley, Chris Morris, Flaget Nally, Steve and Donna Nally, Denise Naughton, Ken Newbaker, Booker Noe, H. Edward O'Daniel Jr., Bob O'Halloran, F. Paul Pacult, Mike Polisky, Mike Pommer, Henry Price, Mary McGuire Ruggiero, Jimmy Russell, Jim Rutledge, Bill Samuels Jr., Nancy Samuels, Bob Schecter, Max Shapira, Martin Slattery, Thom Smith, Stanley Stankiwicz, Keith Steer, Jerry Summers, Sheila Swerling-Puritt, Meg Syberg, Julian Van Winkle III, Mike Veach, John Vidal, Chris Willis, Sue Woodley, Michael Wright, Al Young.

ILLUSTRATION AND PHOTO CREDITS

Front cover photograph by: Michael Weiss
Back flap photograph of authors by:
Lisa Koenig

p. 5: Statue of Colonel Albert B. Blanton.
Courtesy of the Ancient Age Distillery,
Frankfort, Kentucky.

p. 7: Old Kentucky distillery. Collection of
the authors.

p. 8: ©Tria Giovan. T. William Samuels Jr.'s
bourbon bottle collection. Courtesy of
Maker's Mark Distillery, Loretto, Kentucky.

p. 10: Moving a barrel. Courtesy of United
Distillers North American Archives,
Louisville, Kentucky.

p. 13: Crystal Springs Distillery circa 1886.
Courtesy of Seagram's Four Roses Distillery,
Lawrenceburg, Kentucky.

p. 15: Elijah Craig. Courtesy of Heaven Hill
Distillery, Bardstown, Kentucky.

p. 16: ©Dan Dry. Edge of cypress
fermenter. Courtesy of Maker's Mark
Distillery, Loretto, Kentucky.

p. 18: Doubler at Stitzel-Weller, circa 1975.
Courtesy of United Distillers North
American Archives, Louisville, Kentucky.

p. 19: A mash tub. Courtesy of Maker's
Mark Distillery, Loretto, Kentucky.

p. 20: The charcoal mellowing process.
Courtesy of the Jack Daniel Distillery,
Lynchburg, Tennessee.

p. 21: Burning ricks of sugar maple for
charcoal. Courtesy of the Jack Daniel
Distillery, Lynchburg, Tennessee.

p. 22: ©Dan Dry. Sampling a barrel of
Maker's Mark. Courtesy of Maker's Mark
Distillery, Loretto, Kentucky.

p. 23: Evan Williams Single-Barrel Vintage
1989 Bourbon. Courtesy of Heaven Hill
Distillery, Bardstown, Kentucky.

p. 25: Food-grade corn. Courtesy of the Jack
Daniel Distillery, Lynchburg, Tennessee.

p. 26: Antique yeast cooler in the Oscar
Getz Museum of Whiskey History,
Bardstown, Kentucky. Collection of the
authors.

p. 27: Shipping dock of the Old Fitzgerald
Distillery. Courtesy of United Distillers
North American Archives, Louisville,
Kentucky.

p. 28: Charcoal mellowing tanks. Courtesy
of the Jack Daniel Distillery, Lynchburg,
Tennessee.

p. 29: Sugar-maple charcoal. Courtesy of
the Jack Daniel Distillery, Lynchburg,
Tennessee.

p. 31: The Yellowstone/Taylor & Williams

Distillery, circa 1900. Courtesy of United
Distillers North American Archives,
Louisville, Kentucky.

p. 32–33: Diagram courtesy of United
Distillers North American Archives,
Louisville, Kentucky.

p. 33: A grain cooker at Maker's Mark.
Courtesy of Maker's Mark Distillery,
Loretto, Kentucky.

p. 34: Jacob's Well Whiskey made by Jim
Beam Brands, Clermont, Kentucky.

p. 37: ©Bruce Curtis

p. 38: ©Bruce Curtis

p. 39: ©Bruce Curtis

p. 40: ©Bruce Curtis

p. 42: James F. Pepper advertisement.
Courtesy of United Distillers North
American Archives, Louisville, Kentucky.

p. 44: Old Charter advertisement, circa
1973. Courtesy of United Distillers North
American Archives, Louisville, Kentucky.

p. 142: A truckload of barrels. Courtesy of
the Jack Daniel Distillery, Lynchburg,
Tennessee.

p. 145: Elmer T. Lee, Master Distiller
Emeritus. Courtesy of the Ancient Age
Distillery, Frankfort, Kentucky.

p. 147: Single-barrel bottling house.
Courtesy of the Ancient Age Distillery,
Frankfort, Kentucky.

p. 148: ©Bobbe Wolf. The bottling line.
Courtesy of Barton Brands, Bardstown,
Kentucky.

p. 149: The Bernheim Distillery. Courtesy
of United Distillers North American
Archives, Louisville, Kentucky.

p. 151: Label of Old Forester Bourbon
made at Brown-Forman's Early Times
Distillery, Louisville, Kentucky.

p. 152: The Four Roses Distillery. Courtesy
of Seagram's Four Roses Archives,
Lawrenceburg, Kentucky.

p. 155: Heaven Hill Springs Distillery, circa
1935. Courtesy of Heaven Hill Distillery,
Bardstown, Kentucky.

p. 157: Barrels to the warehouse. Courtesy
of the Jack Daniel Distillery, Lynchburg,
Tennessee.

p. 163: ©William Strode. The Maker's Mark
Distillery. Courtesy of Maker's Mark
Distillery, Loretto, Kentucky.

p. 164: ©Clark Capps. Courtesy of the
Sazerac Company, New Orleans, Louisiana.

p. 166: The Oscar Getz Museum of
Whiskey History, Bardstown, Kentucky.
Collection of the authors.

INDEX

PERSONAL TASTING NOTES

LABEL:

STYLE:

BATCH YEAR:

DATE TASTED:

RATING (1–100):

COMMENTS:

LABEL:

STYLE:

BATCH YEAR:

DATE TASTED:

RATING (1–100):

COMMENTS:

LABEL:

STYLE:

BATCH YEAR:

DATE TASTED:

RATING (1–100):

COMMENTS:

LABEL:

STYLE:

BATCH YEAR:

DATE TASTED:

RATING (1–100):

COMMENTS:

LABEL:

STYLE:

BATCH YEAR:

DATE TASTED:

RATING (1–100):

COMMENTS:

LABEL:

STYLE:

BATCH YEAR:

DATE TASTED:

RATING (1–100):

COMMENTS:

LABEL:

STYLE:

BATCH YEAR:

DATE TASTED:

RATING (1–100):

COMMENTS:

LABEL:

STYLE:

BATCH YEAR:

DATE TASTED:

RATING (1–100):

COMMENTS:

LABEL:

STYLE:

BATCH YEAR:

DATE TASTED:

RATING (1–100):

COMMENTS:

LABEL:

STYLE:

BATCH YEAR:

DATE TASTED:

RATING (1–100):

COMMENTS:

LABEL:

STYLE:

BATCH YEAR:

DATE TASTED:

RATING (1–100):

COMMENTS:

LABEL:

STYLE:

BATCH YEAR:

DATE TASTED:

RATING (1–100):

COMMENTS: